Here's What They're Saying . . .

"This book, densely packed with wisdom to live by, offers a much-needed look into the process of recovery and spirituality. . . . It addresses the commonly ignored but prevalent problem of 'hitting bottom sober.' The author is a wonderful teacher and storyteller who believes in, and writes about, transformation."

—Judith G. Dowling, Psy.D.
clinical psychologist

"I plan to give a copy of this book, instead of a prescription for Prozac, to my patients who are seeking this path."

—Dawn V. Obrecht, M.D., P.C.
family medicine, addictive diseases

"Through the minefield of despair and the many dark nights that often occur during recovery, this book leads us to new heights of spiritual understanding. Highly recommended."

—Bill Cox, M.D.
Lutheran Medical Center

"A masterful job of presenting all the issues—resistance, denial and dogged persistence—required for this marvelous journey. It will be required reading for my recovering clients as they shore up their 12-Step foundation to support stage two therapeutic work."

—Mary Roush, M.S., LPC, NCC, CACIII
psychotherapist

D0197679

The DARK NIGHT of RECOVERY

Conversations from the Bottom of the Bottle

Edward Bear

Health Communications, Inc.
Deerfield Beach, Florida

www.bcibooks.com

Library of Congress Cataloging-in-Publication Data

Bear, Edward, date.
    The dark night of recovery: conversations from the bottom of the
bottle/Edward Bear.
        p.   cm.
    ISBN-13: 978-1-55874-653-4 (trade paper)
    ISBN-10: 1-55874-653-6 (trade paper)
        1. Alcoholics—Rehabilitation—Fiction.   2. Imaginary conversations.
    3. Spiritual life—Fiction. I. Title.
    PS3552.E156D37 1999
    813'.54—dc21   98-43235
                                                                              CIP

Publisher: Health Communications, Inc.
              3201 S.W. 15th Street
              Deerfield Beach, FL 33442-8190

To Jo, who makes the forest green.

The children—Tom, Tree, Cat, Monica, Laura and Steve.

My sister, Mike. My brother, Gene.

Judith, my cosmic twin and muse.

Dan, for all the right reasons.

Linda Roghaar, for being the best of agents.

All those most likely to answer the phone at midnight and show up at the barricades when requested (you know who you are).

In the real dark night of the soul, it's always three o'clock in the morning.

—F. Scott Fitzgerald

The eye with which you see God is the same eye with which God sees you.

—Meister Eckhart

There is no companion but love.
No starting or finishing, yet a Road.
The Friend calls from There:
Why do you hesitate when lives are in danger!

—Rumi

Every day people are straying away from the church and going back to God.

—Lenny Bruce

This is serious, said Pooh. I must have an escape.

—Winnie-the-Pooh

Where there is no love, put love and you will find love.

—St. Francis

CONTENTS

THE TWELVE STEPS OF ALCOHOLICS ANONYMOUS

1. We admitted we were powerless over alcohol—that our lives had become unmanageable.
2. Came to believe that a Power greater than ourselves could restore us to sanity.
3. Made a decision to turn our will and our lives over to the care of God *as we understood Him*.
4. Made a searching and fearless moral inventory of ourselves.
5. Admitted to God, to ourselves and to another human being the exact nature of our wrongs.
6. Were entirely ready to have God remove all these defects of character.
7. Humbly asked Him to remove our shortcomings.

8. Made a list of all persons we had harmed, and became willing to make amends to them all.

9. Made direct amends to such people whenever possible, except when to do so would injure them or others.

10. Continued to take personal inventory and when we were wrong promptly admitted it.

11. Sought through prayer and meditation to improve our conscious contact with God, *as we understood Him,* praying only for knowledge of His will for us and the power to carry that out.

12. Having had a spiritual awakening as a result of these steps, we tried to carry this message to alcoholics, and to practice these principles in all our affairs.

PROLOGUE

Most everybody knew old Tyler. He'd been hanging around the Westside Alano club for as long as anyone could remember. Had a face looked like somebody forgot to water it; dry as an old boot, roadmapped with wrinkles, the face of a man who'd spent a good deal of time looking at horizons.

Lawyer Bob was the guy who wore the Armani suits, had the House on the Hill, the Big Job. Had it all. Everybody figured him for Mister Success. Huh. Little did they know. He had a hole in his life the size of a suitcase. Bob was the one told me the story about how he and Tyler got together a year or so ago when Bob was having all that trouble. You know the drill—Famine, Pestilence, Death, Romance and Finance. Divorce and Financial Ruin. You'd think a lawyer would know better. Anyway, he went to Tyler because he figured that anyone with thirty years in recovery ought to have some answers. First thing Tyler told him was he didn't have any answers. First thing; like he was reading his mind. Then he went on.

"Sounds like you're about to enter the dark part of the forest. The part where the real work begins. You ready to go back to school?"

"I did the steps already," said Bob.

"Good. Once more won't hurt. And try not to be defensive. I'm on your side."

"I'm not being defensive."

"You're being defensive," said Tyler. "Trust me on this; I know defensive when I see it. Now, it would seem that the preliminary work is done—you have hit bottom sober. Very important. And now you are about to enter the Dark Night, the Great Desert, where you will either fall by the wayside and die, go mad, or survive and experience real recovery."

"Those are the only choices?"

"All spiritual journeys contain elements of death and transfiguration. Recovery's no different. It's just part of the deal."

"Sounds like major surgery," said Bob.

"True. But the alternative is to stop growing and join those who linger in that gray limbo of semi-recovery, not drinking or using or feeding their other addictions, but not really living either, dispensing Advice and Tough Love to defenseless newcomers, glumly counting birthdays as if the sheer number might guarantee a certain amount of happiness. You want that?"

"No."

"You want to be free?"

"I want to be free."

"Good. We may be on to something here. How about we meet at your place every other Tuesday? Seven o'clock. You have a tape recorder?"

"Yeah."

"Good. Get some tapes. Long ones."

"Why the tapes?"

"Mostly to humor an old man," said Tyler. "And someday you may want to remember what it was like. You may even want to *tell* somebody what it was like. It'll help you refresh your memory."

Bob said he tried to explain some of his numerous problems to Tyler that night, but Tyler wouldn't listen.

"You've just got one problem, counselor. You're addicted to a wide variety of things, most notably alcohol, and that addiction, that state of dis-ease, results in a pathological obsession with self, a condition needlessly prolonged by your desire to figure it out. Figure-it-out-ism is itself a disease nearly always fatal in advanced cases. Like yours. Often leads to what's-the-use-ism or poor-me-ism, both known to be terminal in addicts of all kinds. What you really have is a surrender problem."

"A surrender problem?"

"I'll explain later. For your first assignment, read up to page forty-five in the Big Book and explain what powerless means. Read Step One in the Twelve and Twelve. Read *The House at Pooh Corner* and write down the most important passage."

"*The House at Pooh Corner?*"

"As in Winnie-the-Pooh," said Tyler.

"The most important passage in the whole book?"

"It's not *War and Peace*, Bob. It's just a little book. And read chapter 71 in the *Tao Te Ching* and tell me how it relates to the First Step."

"Tyler . . ."

"And that's just the beginning. It's like life—the lessons just keep coming. Suit up and show up and be ready. And one other thing."

"Yeah?"

"Try smiling once in a while. It's just life. Far as I know, nobody's getting out of this thing alive. Might as well enjoy the journey. See you in two weeks?"

"I'll be there."

"And so will I. Fasten your seat belt, counselor; you are about to embark on the journey of your life."

Bob asked me if I'd transcribe the tapes, me being a writer and all. Two articles in the local paper and I'm a writer. Of course, I don't discourage the notion. So here they are—The Tyler Tapes (with only slight editing by yours truly). Bob says they saved his life. See what you think.

Step One

"Well, what did you discover about the First Step?" said Tyler.

"I wrote some stuff down," said Bob.

"Good. First read the step. Out loud."

"Admitted we were powerless over alcohol, that our lives had become unmanageable."

"First word is *we*," said Tyler. *"We* admitted we were powerless. This is a *we* deal."

"Right," said Bob. "We."

"And the stuff you wrote down?"

"Oh, just some notes. A few quotes."

"That all?"

"Yeah."

"You mean it's not perfect?"

"Hardly," said Bob.

1

"I've got another assignment for you," said Tyler. "Better write it down so you don't forget it. There's a book that starts out, 'The only sin is self-hatred.' First sentence. Find it and read it."

"Tyler, how in the world am I ever going to find a book from just the first sentence?"

"You'll find a way. Better yet, a way will be provided. The steps will teach you about finding answers when there are no answers. About a Higher Power. About synchronicity. You know about synchronicity?"

"Sure," said Bob. "Meaningful coincidence."

"Hey, who said lawyers weren't smart? You will begin to know things you have no way of knowing. People will begin to show up in your life when you need them. People. Things. They just show up. It's amazing. A way will always be provided."

"How come I don't know this stuff already? I've been around almost five years."

"You were being properly aged," said Tyler. "Prepared. Seasoned. You weren't quite ready."

"And I am now?"

"Seems like. I'm an expert on pain. When people get teachable, I can tell."

"Huh. So now I'm ready and waiting," said Bob. "For a way. For *the* way."

"And for the magic."

"Great. My life is turning to Shinola even as we speak and I'm waiting for the magic."

"Better yet," said Tyler, "the magic and the symphony. The music of sobriety. Of recovery. The voices. You ever go to a meeting in some out-of-the-way place where you don't know anybody? One of those rooms where the curtains are so old they're yellow and the place smells like a dirty ashtray? Some little town in Montana maybe. Wyoming. Cowboys and ranchers—a grim group. You don't know anybody and you're sorry you went. Should'a stayed at the motel and watched the movie on TV. Lousy movie but better than this. Then the meeting starts. The magic. The voices: *'Rarely have we seen a person fail.'* The melody: *'I'm Charley and I'm . . .'* Every meeting has a Charley. The symphony of sobriety. Doesn't take long to realize that you're in the Right Place."

"The magic . . . and the music," said Bob.

"Right."

"And just what does all this have to do with the First Step?"

"Everything," said Tyler. "We're beginning at the beginning. Step One. You have to understand the lineage—AA's spiritual heritage. *Your* spiritual heritage. It starts with Carl Jung. Synchronicity—that's his. From Jung we get a guy named Roland who returns to a Christian congregation called the Oxford Group with Jung's message that his—Roland's—alcoholism will end in either death or insanity unless he experiences a spiritual conversion of some kind. Bill W. calls that message the first link in the chain that eventually led to the founding of Alcoholics Anonymous. Bill's friend, Ebby, goes to see him during the worst of his drinking, brings him the Oxford Group message about restitution, self-disclosure and service to others, tells him how it's keeping him sober. Bill says, 'Yeah, yeah, yeah, sounds good,' but drinks again and ends up in Towns Hospital with the familiar Dr. Silkworth. Old Silky. There, he has the spiritual experience that relieves him of his compulsion to drink. Then he reads *Varieties of Religious Experience* and realizes that most spiritual conversions are born of a deep sense of despair; the deeper the better. Hence the emphasis on powerlessness in the First Step. The alcoholic or addict must be convinced that he is powerless, that his condition is an absolute no-hoper, that his life goes in the tank the minute he takes that first drink." He paused. "Were you a bad drunk?"

"Terrible," said Bob.

"You did some terrible things?"

"Awful."

"Like what?" said Tyler.

"I've been known to take a whiz in an elevator from time to time. Crowded usually. It's almost like I didn't want to waste the effort without an audience. Crazy."

"A marginal case. I know real crazy when I hear it."

"Once I was in L.A. leaving a dance at the Miramar Hotel and I stopped to christen a palm tree. In my tuxedo yet."

"At least you were dressed for the occasion."

"Yeah."

"You Yale guys are a classy bunch," said Tyler.

"You know other Yale drunks?"

"Actually only one. Yale law, just like you. Dead now."

"Oh?"

"Yeah. Smart guy. Really smart. Probably one of the smartest guys I ever met. Never did seem to understand about alcoholism, though, about not drinking one day at a time. Maybe it was too simple for him. Let me read you something from one of the Pooh books."

"What is it with you and Winnie-the-Pooh?" said Bob.

"Pooh was very wise," said Tyler. "You probably should have been studying Pooh at Yale instead of poring over all those hundred-dollar textbooks every night."

"Sorry I interrupted."

"Apology accepted. This is Pooh talking to Piglet:

"*'Rabbit's clever,' said Pooh.*

'Yes,' said Piglet. 'Rabbit's clever. And he has a brain.'

'I suppose,' said Pooh, 'that's why he never understands anything.'"

"So the guy from Yale had a brain," said Bob.

"The worst possible kind—a Big Brain," said Tyler. "Smart guy. A figure-it-out guy. Like you. Bright."

"Big Brain didn't help?"

"No. Big Brains think too much. Sobriety is a language of the heart. Big Brains make way too much noise; can't hear the heart. The whispers."

"What's the message?" said Bob.

"It's hard to learn when you already know everything. Now, back to lesson one. What does powerless mean?"

"I looked it up in the dictionary."

"Typical college trick," said Tyler. "But acceptable in this case."

"Since power means having control and influence over something or someone, powerless means being without control, without influence, zip."

"Not bad. Out of control—I'll buy that. What does the Big Book say?"

"*We are without defense against the first drink.*"

"Defenseless," said Tyler.

"Powerless."

"Good. And . . . ?"

"Defense must come from a higher power."

"Interesting development. And the Twelve and Twelve?"

"Our admission of powerlessness is the bedrock on which a happy and purposeful life may be built."

"Imagine that," said Tyler. "A happy and purposeful life. What a deal. Those notes you took aren't bad at all, counselor. Now, on to *The House at Pooh Corner.*"

"I don't get all this stuff about Winnie-the-Pooh."

"You will. Give it time."

"I picked the three most important passages from it," said Bob.

"Very alcoholic," said Tyler. "Getting three when one will do. Pick one and read it."

"Okay, try this. You'll be proud of me."

"I'm already proud of you."

"You are?"

"Read," said Tyler.

"Okay . . . this is Rabbit talking:"

"'You can't help respecting anybody who can spell TUESDAY even if he doesn't spell it right. Spelling isn't everything. There are days when spelling TUESDAY simply doesn't count.'"

"Translation?" said Tyler.

"There are days when spelling Tuesday and being smart and having a law degree from Yale don't count."

"What does count?"

"Being sober?"

"You asking me?"

"No. Being sober. Period."

"Not bad," said Tyler.

"You got a better one?"

"You know I do. This is when Pooh and Piglet are lost in the woods:

"Pooh looked at his two paws. He knew that one of them was right, and he knew that when he decided which was the right one, the other would be the left ... but he could never remember how to begin."

"Very ... obtuse," said Bob.

"Obtuse my ass," said Tyler. "Perfect Step One position of powerlessness. The Dilemma: How to begin? Once you admit you're powerless over alcohol and its companion drugs, that your life is unmanageable, you've identified the right hand."

"And then do we get to hear the sound of one hand clapping?"

Tyler ignored that. "Then you know the other hand is the left, the other foot is the left and you have a place to begin. One foot in front of the other. Right, left, right, left. Trudging the Road of Happy Destiny. The Road of Recovery. The Tao."

"Jesus," said Bob, "the Tao. At last."

"Stop listening with your brain."

"I'm trying."

"Remember what Yoda says about trying."

"Who's Yoda?" said Bob.

"*Star Wars* Yoda," said Tyler. "The Jedi Master. He said, 'Try not. Do. Or do not. There is no try.'"

"I'll keep that in mind."

"Do. Now read chapter 71 in the Tao."

"To realize that our knowledge is ignorance,
This is a noble insight.
To regard our ignorance as knowledge,
This is mental sickness.
Only when we are sick of sickness
Shall we cease to be sick."

"Explanation?" said Tyler.

"I've got it here somewhere. Here it is, page thirty-nine: *The alcoholic, with hardly an exception, will be unable to stop drinking on the basis of self knowledge.*"

"Well done, counselor," said Tyler. "Ties it all up nicely. When you're really sick and tired of being sick and tired, you may be able to suspend your judgment and listen. Maybe even begin to get well. See how it all fits?"

[A long silence with only tape hiss in the background.]

"See how it fits?" Tyler repeated.

"I can't do this anymore," said Bob. "This is crazy. My life is turning to shit and we're into being sick and tired of being sick and tired. Word games. Not to mention Winnie the god-damn Pooh and *Star Wars'* Yoda. Jesus, Tyler. My wife is leaving me, for chrissakes. She's walking out."

"A side issue," said Tyler.

"A *side* issue? We've been married for eighteen years and you think this is a *side* issue?"

"Hey, you're not the person she married."

"I'm *better* than the person she married. Lots better."

"I didn't say you weren't better. I just said you're not the man she married. You changed. That's not her fault."

"She always wanted me to get sober," said Bob. "Right from the beginning. She nagged me about it. Now I'm sober."

"Maybe she doesn't like you sober."

"I can't believe you said that."

"What's your number one problem?"

"You guys are all the same," said Bob. "You know that? You get a few years in and it's all clichés and platitudes. You forget. You forget what it's like to struggle, to be young, to have something going for you. You have these things you say, these . . . *things* that are supposed to mean something because you're thirty years into recovery. It's blah, blah, blah. Stupid clichés."

"And your number one problem is?"

"You!" he shouted.

"We'll try again," said Tyler. "Your number one problem . . . ?"

"Ahhhhhh." Like air going out of a balloon. "God, I hate this. My number one problem is alcohol."

"No."

"No?"

"Alcohol is a neutral substance, counselor. It's like water, Pepsi, Gatorade. It's neutral. Your real problem is . . . ?"

"I'm an alcoholic," said Bob, defeat in his voice.

"Good," Tyler said cheerfully. "Always good to identify the source of the problem. That's a good start."

"This is a good start?"

"Of course. You're angry and frustrated. The old ways don't work anymore and you don't really have any new ones yet. At least none that you could use. You've hit bottom sober. *Thud!* Flat as a pancake. Living sober has beaten you into a state of reasonableness. It's perfect. The Universe is conspiring to heal you, to help you get rid of a lot of excess baggage. You're totally helpless. Your life is trash. Even you must be able to see that it's unmanageable."

"Even me," said Bob.

"Even you. Bulletproof Bob."

"You're killin' me, Tyler. You know that?"

"Only the old you. And I am leading you through the dark part of the forest. We clear on Step One?"

"Crystal."

"Just remember that the map is not the territory. The menu is not the meal. We've got too many people eating the menu, thinking it's dinner. The menu just tells you what's available. Don't eat it."

"What's that supposed to mean?"

"Think about it," said Tyler. "It'll come to you. Ready for your next assignment?"

"I guess. I'm not liking this, Tyler. Not at all."

"I'd be worried if you were. Read up to page sixty in the Big Book and tell me what insanity means to you. Read the Second Step in the Twelve and Twelve. Read *The Empire Strikes Back* and let me know what Yoda has to say about Step Two. Also pages forty-nine to seventy-seven in *Alcoholics Anonymous Comes of Age* and chapter 41 in the Tao."

"That all?" said Bob sarcastically.

"You want more?"

"No *Winnie-the-Pooh* this time?"

"We could—"

"Never mind."

"Remember that this is a spiritual journey," said Tyler. "Much of it takes place in the darkness. You will have to keep moving when you would much rather lie down and die. The road will get very narrow. You will want to turn back. Don't. You will know the worst loneliness of your life, but you will never be alone. In the immortal words of Tigger, when he first saw his reflection in a mirror: 'Hello . . . I've found somebody just like me. And I thought I was the only one of them.'"

"Great," said Bob. "Pooh and now Tigger with words of wisdom. Welcome to school, children."

"Say that again," said Tyler.

"Pooh and now Tigger."

"No, the last part," said Tyler.

"'Welcome to school, children'?"

"That's it. Perfect. Welcome to school, children."

"Nobody told me about this part, Tyler. About how it would be."

"It's not this way for everyone. Some don't get this far. Some quit. Some drink or use or O.D. on chocolate cake. Some die. Some decide it's not worth it. And of course the gifts you receive are not for you alone. I will just say that the time will come when you will be grateful for the experience."

"Not today, though?"

"And probably not tomorrow," said Tyler.

"The day after?"

"Very alcoholic, counselor. Projections. Lesson two has to do with beliefs. Very interesting stuff: *Came to believe that a Power greater than ourselves could restore us to sanity.* You have two weeks to prepare."

"Jesus. Two weeks—I could be dead in two weeks."

"No such luck, counselor. You only get to leave when your work is done."

"And mine's not?"

"Oh, no. Yours is just beginning."

"Jesus."

Step Two

"How goes it?" said Tyler.

"I've had better days," said Bob. "Lots better. Better whole weeks as a matter of fact. I have to be out of the house by November first."

"*You* have to be out of the house?"

"Looks like."

"You need a better lawyer."

"Very funny."

"On the road again," said Tyler. "A familiar refrain."

"My own house and I have to leave."

"Good riddance to that house, counselor. Good riddance. You don't need it."

"How do you know I don't need it? Turns out I *do* need that house. Lots of my . . . energy is tied up in that house."

"Not to mention your money."

"Of course my money. It's not a crime to have money. Even in AA, where it seems much more acceptable to be broke and miserable."

"Your life is beginning to reflect your journey," said Tyler. "Not all that surprising. Perhaps you need to be alone for a time, away from everything familiar, everything comfortable."

"So God is removing things just in case I forget to lighten the load?"

"Maybe. Your birthday coming up soon? Your sobriety anniversary?"

"November eleventh. If I live that long."

"Perfect," said Tyler. "You'll be five years clean and sober on Armistice Day. Surrender Day. And by that time you'll have finished your Fifth Step."

"Oh, boy," said Bob, clapping his hands. "I'm underwhelmed. My birthday and the Fifth Step. My life will be complete. We'll celebrate. We'll have cake and ice cream."

"More likely dust and ashes," said Tyler. "The fruits of a spiritual journey."

"I'd rather have cake and ice cream."

"Wouldn't we all."

"You know, I'm forty-five years old, Tyler. Forty-five and I'm not getting anywhere. Going anywhere. Most people my age are established, or at least on their way up. I'm headed the other way. Down the tubes. I hate to say this, but I was doing better when I was drinking."

"Maybe you never should have stopped," said Tyler. "If you'd kept at it, who knows, you might be president of General Motors by now."

"Well, there were some problems."

"Oh?"

"Some . . . fairly serious, actually. How old were you when you got sober?"

"Thirty-five."

"You still had a job?"

"I had my parole papers, my Smiling-Frankie-Gordon thirty-dollar suit, a small paycheck that only my parole officer could cash, and a promise of a minimum-wage job."

"But you made it."

"I had some added incentives. When things were bad, I thought about the bull in South Block who told me, 'You'll be back, Tyler. Guys like you can't make it out there.' And the guard at the gate who said, 'You want a tip, convict? Don't wear that coat in the rain. Ha ha ha.' Yeah, I made it. I'm a survivor. So are you."

"You have a hard time?"

"As I recall," said Tyler, "my worst year on the planet was my fifth or sixth year sober. Maybe the seventh. Maybe all three. Anyway, it wasn't pretty. I hit the wall sober and didn't know what to do."

"I don't find that encouraging."

"Look on the bright side—I'm still here. Let me remind you that it's a process. It takes time. Most of us are not long on patience."

"I'll consider myself reminded."

"I have something instructive here written by Thomas Merton. It's about the journey."

"How long you been collecting things in that notebook?"

"Long time. Started because I could never remember all the good things I read. Too many books. Lousy memory. So

I took all the good quotes and put them in this notebook. Listen to this. It's from *The Seven Story Mountain.* Thomas Merton. God is talking to Merton."

"Why doesn't God talk to me?" said Bob.

"Maybe he does. Maybe you don't listen. Here's what he says to Merton:

"I will lead you into solitude. I will lead you by the way that you cannot understand because I want it to be the quickest way. . . . All things will be armed against you, to deny you, to reduce you to solitude."

"Sounds like a slam dunk by the Big Guy," said Bob. "You know, I just checked the score, Tyler."

"Of what?"

"Of the Game. The Life Game."

"And?"

"It's God, ninety-three; mankind, zip. Nada. And it's not even halftime yet."

"Don't worry—we're a second-half team."

"I hope," said Bob. "But I don't know if it makes any difference anyway because I'm not sure I even *believe* in God."

"Not required," said Tyler.

"Not required for what?"

"For membership. For the journey. Simply not required."

"You know I came here as one of the true believers," said Bob. "I was raised Catholic."

"Everybody was raised Catholic," said Tyler. "I remember the drill—Hangover, Confession, Mass, Communion, Hangover, Confession . . ."

"Yeah."

"Big Book says you just have to be willing to believe," said

Tyler. "Just willing. That's enough. There are real live athe-
ists in recovery doing very well, thank you. This is not about
religion."

"I *was* willing. I *did* believe. What did it get me?"

"Your very best efforts got you to the doors of Alcoholics
Anonymous. Your very best. Remember that when we start
talking about surrender."

"Jesus. I don't get it."

"How about, 'Came to believe that the Great Pumpkin could
restore us to sanity'? That sound better? Less threatening?"

"I'm not threatened by the God thing, Tyler. I don't even
believe in God." Bob paused. "Who's the Great Pumpkin?"

"*Peanuts?* Charlie Brown? Didn't they teach you anything
worthwhile at Yale? Every Halloween Linus and Snoopy go
out to the pumpkin patch to wait for the Great Pumpkin,
who traditionally rises from the pumpkin patch he thinks is
the most sincere."

"My, my. The most sincere pumpkin patch."

"Right. Then he flies off and brings toys to all the good
children in the world."

"He flies? This pumpkin?"

"Yep."

"Like Santa Claus?"

"Sort of. I don't think he's got a sleigh and reindeer. I
always hated it that you had to be good to get toys. Like it
was blackmail. Whatever happened to unconditional love?"

"But he never comes to the pumpkin patch where Linus
and Snoopy are waiting?"

"Hasn't yet."

"But he will someday?"

"That's what Linus and Snoopy believe."

"You think that's rational?" said Bob. "Waiting for something that only just might happen. Probably won't. I mean, when you consider all the pumpkin patches in the world . . ."

"Of course, it's not rational. Who said anything about being rational? It's about hope. You're using your Big Brain again, counselor. Very risky."

"Turn off the Big Brain."

"Right," said Tyler. "And on with Step Two. I'm going to quote some things out of the Big Book and the Twelve and Twelve and I want you to tell me which one it's from."

"This a test? You want to know if I did my reading?"

"I want to know if you've done your studying. The cover on the Big Book says it's the basic text, as in textbook. As in study. Ready?"

"Shoot."

"Alcohol finally beat us into a state of reasonableness."

"The Big Book."

"Good. *Circumstances made him willing to believe.*"

"The Twelve and Twelve."

"Nope," said Tyler. "The Big Book. *Defiance is the outstanding characteristic of many an alcoholic.*"

"You make this stuff up as you go along?" said Bob.

"No. I'll assume you don't have a clue about where that came from. Try this one: *Nearly all spiritual experiences have the common denominators of pain, suffering and calamity.*"

"How about the Big Book?"

"No. *Alcoholics Anonymous Comes of Age.*"

"Tyler, you said the Big Book or the Twelve and . . ."

"Do I sense some resistance here, counselor? If this is too hard for you, let me know. I don't want to be wasting your time. Or mine."

"No. It's just that I don't *get* it."

"Not important that you *get* it. It's only important that you *do* it. And if you're going to *do* it, it has to be done a certain way."

"Meaning your way, of course," said Bob. "And what is it that happens to be so good about your way?"

"It's so good because it's not *your* way," said Tyler. "Your way doesn't work. If it did, we wouldn't be sitting here having this conversation. You have a defective thinker. A defective, Yale-educated thinker—much worse than a normal defective thinker, and unless you stop trying to figure it out, stop trying to think your way into recovery, you're going to die. Die, counselor. D-i-e. Not quickly and mercifully, which might not be all that bad, but slowly, painfully, with plenty of time to think about it. It is a known fact that you can only act your way into recovery. Suspend your judgment for now; it's not doing you much good anyway."

"Shit, Tyler."

"Defiance is the outstanding characteristic of just about every alcoholic or addict I ever met."

"Ahhh."

"It says in the book," said Tyler. "Listen now: *Do I now believe, or am I willing to believe, that there is a power greater than myself?*"

"I guess so," Bob mumbled.

"You guess so?"

"I would say that I am willing, but just barely," said Bob. "That's the best I can do."

"Doesn't specify degrees of willingness," said Tyler. "Somebody once said that surrender was getting well somebody else's way. Doesn't make any difference who, as long as it's not you."

"Another gem of wisdom from a derelict."

"Yet another," said Tyler. "How many can there be?"

"You could maybe do a book on it: *Gems of Wisdom from Hopeless Derelicts.*"

"Maybe later. Here's what I heard about the Second Step when I first came around: 'We came. We came to. And finally, we came to believe that a power greater than ourselves could restore us to sanity.' You understand what insanity means?"

"The evidence is in."

"I don't mean bizarre. Peeing in elevators and on palm trees is bizarre behavior. Insanity is taking that first drink if you're an alcoholic, thinking maybe it wasn't really so bad after all, ingesting painkillers for phantom back pains if you're a drug addict, having just one jelly doughnut if you're an overeater, betting a few dollars on a football game if your primary addiction is gambling. The list goes on. Insanity is always self-destructive, though others often get hurt in the process. Those people you hate out there? The ones who are always in-the-way and complicating your life? They're just you in different clothes, cleverly disguised as Other People. They are lessons. They will keep showing up until you learn the lesson. When you're through with this part of the process, you'll understand more about that."

Tyler paused a beat, then two. "You want to know what you believe about life, look around you. See what you've attracted. What's in your life is what you believe. It's possible you believe in sickness more than health, in conflict more than harmony. What's there is what you believe. It's not about right or wrong. Your beliefs about what is possible determine what is possible. Spend some time on this step— it begins the process of altering beliefs. Very powerful. Am I getting through?"

"I hear you. It's just that there's so much crap going on in my life."

"Money, property and prestige."

"I know, I know, but it's *real*, Tyler. It's right in my face twenty-four hours a day and I can't reduce it to words and make it go away."

"I know it's hard," said Tyler. "Believe me, I know that. Try to think of time as your ally, not your enemy."

"Tyler, I'm forty-five years old."

"Time is your ally, Bob. Your ally."

"But . . ."

"Your ally."

"Okay."

"Good. Let's do the Tao and finish up with Yoda. You read *The Empire Strikes Back*?"

"Most of it. I try to save a little time for work."

"Chapter 41 of the Tao?"

"I copied it down."

"Good," said Tyler. "Read."

"'When a man of . . .'"

"Start with, 'The proverb has it.'"

"The Proverb has it that
The way of light often looks dark.
The way that goes forward appears to go backward.
The flat path looks hilly.
The power that is lofty looks like an abyss.
The power that stands firm looks flimsy.
What is in its pure state looks faded.
Great talents ripen late.
Great sound is silent.
Great form is shapeless.

The Tao is hidden and nameless.
Yet it alone knows how to render help and fulfill."

"Meaning?" said Tyler.

"I don't think I get this one," said Bob. "Things are not always what they seem? Expect the unexpected? I'm stuck. It doesn't make sense."

"The Tao is hidden and nameless. The Way is hidden and nameless. How do we find it?"

"Action?"

"Not a bad answer, counselor, especially for someone laboring under the handicap of twenty years of formal education."

"Thanks," said Bob. "Are you at liberty to give me a better answer?"

"Not at the moment."

"But someday?" said Bob.

"By the time I get ready to give you the answer, you'll already know it."

"Jesus."

"How far did you get in *The Empire Strikes Back*?" asked Tyler.

"Almost finished. Luke and Darth Vader are just getting into it."

"And you stopped reading?"

"Fell asleep on the couch. Exhausted. I have been banished to the couch. My wife sleeps with Cyclops the cat."

"Cyclops the cat. Sounds like a Dr. Seuss book. You get through the part where Yoda is trying to teach young Luke Skywalker to become a Jedi Knight?"

"I did."

"And?"

"Luke is very impatient."

"Funny you should notice that."

"I took notes."

"You scholars are always well organized. What was the most important exchange relating to Step Two?"

"I nailed it," said Bob. "Just after Skywalker fails to get his X-wing fighter out of the swamp using the Force, Yoda takes over, lifts it out and sets it on the beach. Skywalker is dumbfounded. He says, 'I don't believe it.' And Yoda says, 'That's why you fail.'"

"Perfect," said Tyler. "Came to believe, counselor."

"An A-plus?" said Bob.

"Don't get carried away. We'll give it a B-plus and call it a vast improvement. You identify any of your own behavior in the last couple of weeks that you'd call insane?"

"Not really."

"Think hard, Mister Bob. Anything at all?"

"Well, I tried to run over the cat the other day. You mean stuff like that?"

"Might qualify. 'Well-known lawyer tries to murder wife's cat.'"

"I hate it when you do that."

"How many meetings you going to?" said Tyler.

"Maybe two a week."

"Not enough. Six a week will be better."

"What with my reading assignments and occasional day at work, I'm a little pressed for time."

"Six. You get one day to do your laundry. You have a service commitment?"

"Sometimes I help clean up after the—"

"Thursday night Mission Meeting needs a coffee maker. The Rusty Zipper Group? Over on Eighth?"

"Jeez, Tyler."

"Ask for Mac. He'll help, show you what to do. They don't get a lot of Yale-educated lawyers down there. You'll be good for them. And of course they'll be good for you. Trust me. You probably have more in common than you think."

"The Rusty Zipper Group. Just my style."

"More than you know, counselor."

"You know, Tyler, sometimes I get a sense of something that's—I don't even know how to describe it—of something that's much . . . bigger than anything I've ever known. I don't know what it is. I don't even know if bigger is the right word. But it goes away almost as soon as I notice it. It's like it's always been there and then I notice it and it's gone. And then I don't even know if it was real to begin with."

"You talk yourself out of it?"

"Maybe. And whatever it is, it seems to be . . . good, maybe?"

"Don't reach for it," said Tyler. "Just watch."

"What is it?"

"Just something from another part of the forest."

"Is it real?" said Bob.

"Later I want you to read *The Velveteen Rabbit,* so you can discover what *real* actually means."

"That a yes or a no?"

"Means you'll figure it out yourself."

"As in time is my ally?"

"Something like that," said Tyler.

"Hope I live that long."

"You will. You have work to do before you move on. Just a few more things. Here's a poem that was found scratched on the wall of a Nazi concentration camp:

"I believe in the sun, even when it isn't shining.
I believe in love, even when I don't feel it.
I believe in God, even when he is silent."

"Painful," said Bob.

"Hopeful," said Tyler.

"The person who wrote that probably died in the gas chamber."

"Probably."

"So what good did it do him?" said Bob. "Believing all that stuff?"

"Everybody leaves the planet someday, Bob. That's not the point."

"Well, what is?"

"I used to drink in a place had this big sign over the back bar: *Free Beer Tomorrow.* Every day I went back expecting free beer, but it was never tomorrow—it was always today.

Took me years to figure that out."

"I'll try again," said Bob. "What *is* the point?"

"The point is that it's always today. Tomorrow is a word invented by some early alcoholic or addict who couldn't deal with today. How you leave the planet is unimportant. The old saying is, God gives the grace of death to the dying. Not to those who are going to die next week or next year. No use trying to get it before you get there. We don't have insurance policies like that. What you believe determines how you live today and all the todays to come. Whether you die in a gas chamber or in a car wreck or in your sleep is not the issue. You going to die today, counselor?"

"I don't think so."

"Good. And besides, nobody ever really dies anyway."

"I won't ask you to explain that," said Bob.

"Because you can't deal with the answer?"

"Maybe. At least not today."

"Hey, I like that," said Tyler.

"You know, this whole thing made much more sense in the first few years. I actually thought I understood some of it then. Now I don't get it. Nothing's the way I thought it would be."

"Never is," said Tyler. "And that's the good news. In the next step we make a decision to turn our will and our lives over to the care of God as we understand him. Step Three. Read up to page sixty-four in the Big Book and Step Three in the Twelve and Twelve. Check chapter 57 in the Tao. And you might as well read *Varieties of Religious Experience* and get that out of the way. You'll see where Bill W. got some of his ideas. And get a book of poetry by Kabir."

"Who?"

"K-a-b-i-r. Sufi mystic and poet. Fifteenth century. Here's a sample:

"Kabir says, only he understands
whose heart and mouth are one."

"I can see why this guy is one of your favorites."

"I may have been a poet in some previous life. 'I'll send the Junkman for your heart.'"

"Kabir?" said Bob.

"No. Line out of a song, I think. Old hearts have to break—it's part of the deal. Let the Junkman come and get it. Your higher power will give you a newer one, a bigger one. You'll need a bigger one for the rest of the journey. More life. More love." There was a slight rustling. "Good night, Bob. Happy trudging. See you in two weeks."

"I hate that line in the Big Book about trudging the Road of Happy Destiny. Hate it."

"Before this is over, you'll learn to love it."

"That's what I'm afraid of. Good night."

Step Three

"I can't sleep," said Bob.

"At all?" said Tyler.

"A little. Few hours a night."

"Couch uncomfortable?"

"Yeah. That and the nightmares."

"Ghosts and goblins?" said Tyler.

"No. Chain saws. Blood. Axes."

"Figures. The ghosts and goblins don't usually show up till the Eighth or Ninth Steps."

"Notice that I'm not laughing," said Bob.

"I'm noticing. Tough couple of weeks?"

"Brutal. You know Donna, my daughter? Sixteen going on thirty. She's acting out."

"Uh-huh. Third Step says that we make a decision to turn

our will and our lives over to the care of God as we understand Him."

"She's threatening to kill herself," said Bob. "What if she
actually does?"

"Then she'll have to come back and do it all over again."

"Do what all over again?"

"Life."

"Tyler . . ."

"Try to remember that everyone has a higher power and
it's not you."

"I'm her father."

"That's nice."

"If she kills herself, I'll never be able to forgive myself."

"She's going to kill herself because of you?" said Tyler.

"Probably," said Bob. "She was brought up in a terrible
household."

"Certainly was. Had a father who spent most of his time
peeing in elevators. Crowded elevators."

"You know what I mean. The fighting, the yelling . . ."

"You consider getting her into therapy?"

"That's the only plus. She started last week."

"She doing okay?"

"She hates it. Hates her therapist. Hates us. Hates
everybody."

"Good. Means she's got spunk."

"Jesus."

"*Made a decision*," said Tyler, "*to turn our will and our
lives over to the care of God as we understood Him.*"

"You're relentless, Tyler. You know that? You probably
never had kids."

"Actually I *do* have kids. Two. Both grown . . ." said Tyler.

"Were three at one time."

"What happened?"

"One died in a car wreck. Jennifer. Hit a tree head on. Big palm tree. Cops figured she must have been going seventy, maybe eighty miles an hour."

"I'm sorry."

"Me, too. Know what I remember most?"

"What?"

"When she was little she had to wear orthopedic shoes. Whenever it rained she'd run outside, take off her shoes and float them in the gutter till they disappeared down the storm drain. Sometimes I can still see her looking into the storm drain as if she expected the shoes to come back. Very expensive shoes. Thirty dollars, I think; lot of money back then. I spanked her every time she did it. Every time. Spanked her hard, too; figured it would teach her a lesson. But it never did. And she never cried. Never. She just looked at me with those big liquid eyes and walked away. She was like clockwork—here comes the rain, there goes Jennifer out the door, and there went the thirty-dollar orthopedic shoes down the drain. That's what I remember. I don't even remember when she graduated from high school. Her big day. I've seen pictures. Maybe I was drunk. Six months later she was gone. Funny, the things you remember."

Tyler cleared his throat. "So," he said. *"Made a decision."*

"Right," said Bob. *"Made a decision."*

"The only thing you can do is work your side of the street, counselor. The only person you can change is you. And when you change, the world changes."

"I hope you know what you're doing, Tyler. There are times when I feel I've placed my life in the hands of a lunatic."

"Lucky you," said Tyler. "And we're just getting warmed up."

"I'm already exhausted."

"Might be a good sign. Might mean you're getting closer to a real surrender."

"I'm ready. Where do I turn in my sword?"

"Ho, ho, ho," said Tyler. "I'm not fooled for a minute. You have a death grip on that sword, counselor. You think that if you can just manage well, or manage at least a little better, everything will be okay."

"What's wrong with managing well?"

"Probably nothing unless you're an alcoholic or an addict," said Tyler. *We are extreme examples of self-will run riot. If people would only do what we wanted, everything would be okay.*"

"That out of the Big Book?"

"You sure you did the steps before?"

"Most of them."

"Driven by a hundred forms of fear, self-delusion and self-pity. Any of that sound familiar?"

"A little."

"Here's the clincher: *So our troubles, we think, are basically of our own making.*"

"Jesus, Tyler. You think I asked for all this crap that's going on in my life?"

"Not relevant, counselor. At least not at the moment. And to answer your first question—the alternative to managing well is Step Three, turning your will and your life over to the care of God as you understand Him. Or Her. Or It. Or God as you *don't* understand Him."

"I don't know," said Bob.

"Let's get back to the Where-do-I-turn-in-my-sword line. Most drunks and addicts have to be on the verge of death before they even consider surrender. And in fact, most of them never do. Most die—car wrecks, heart attacks, cirrhosis, gunshot wounds, overdoses. They never even consider doing it somebody else's way. It's about control, counselor. The need to be in control. To be safe."

"I don't have any control issues," said Bob.

"Alcoholics are men and women who have lost the ability to control their drinking."

"Well, maybe about drinking," said Bob.

"More will be revealed," said Tyler. "But then maybe you're really just a social drinker who had a run of bad luck. You remember why you got into recovery?"

"I . . . couldn't stop drinking. When I started I couldn't stop."

"And you couldn't *not* start."

"Right."

"Sounds like a control problem to me."

"But . . ."

"Look, this step is a no-brainer. Don't spend a lot of time trying to figure it out. Here we can safely fall back on the time-honored spiritual principle of act-as-if. Just do it."

"How?"

"Start with the words. Say the words. Out loud. Say them to a power greater than yourself. To the Great Pumpkin or the Spirit of the Universe. Say them and act-as-if Someone or Something is listening."

"Now I'm an actor," said Bob.

"Right. And you're going to act your way into recovery. The rest comes later."

"It seems so hypocritical."

"You would think that, of course. You would be tuned into that, aware that all this might be tainted with some form of intellectual dishonesty, that it might be just so much spiritual mumbo jumbo." Tyler didn't try to hide his annoyance. "Between times when you were peeing in the elevators you have developed this tremendous sense of intellectual honesty. You're the Show-Me guy. 'Show me it works and then maybe I'll try it.' Doesn't work that way. You have to do it and *then* see if it works. As in action is the magic word. You remember that? You're trying to think your way through it. 'The mind separates. The heart unites'."

"Kabir?"

"Kabir, Joe the Mechanic, Phyllis the Waitress—anyone who's been down the path and experienced it. Pretend you only have one hand."

"Now?"

"Now."

"Okay," said Bob. "I only have one hand. Right hand or left hand?"

"Don't get smart," said Tyler. "I'm going to give you something. Something big."

"Great. It's about time I got a present."

"What's the first thing you do?"

"Say thank you."

"I haven't given it to you yet," said Tyler.

"First thing I do is take it."

"You've already got something in your hand. Your only hand."

"Right away I see we have a problem here. First thing I do is put down the thing that's in my hand?"

"But that thing you already have in your hand is really nice. You've had it all your life. Works pretty well; not great, but pretty well. Doesn't look worn out. Why would you want to put it down when you don't even know what you're going to get?"

"Is this real or make believe?"

"Real as real can be," said Tyler.

"The fact is, I probably wouldn't put it down. Unless you had something absolutely wonderful to replace it."

"How would you find out?"

"Simple. I'd ask you to show me."

"Ah, yes. It's Bob, the Show-Me guy. All I've told you is that it's something big. Could be a dinosaur turd—that's probably big."

"Jesus."

"Understand that control issues are also trust issues, counselor. The finest attribute I brought to this program, that anyone brings to any of the Twelve-Step programs, is a finely honed sense of despair. You have to be desperate. Why else would you be willing to let go of something you've been holding onto all your life? Or do something you've been avoiding for years? Whether you're just getting started, or you're on your way to the next stage of recovery, being desperate counts."

"I certainly must have been desperate," said Bob. "I came

looking for you. Only I couldn't find you. Nobody knew where you were. If only I would have stopped looking when I was ahead. Then one day you just showed up."

"And why me, counselor?"

"People told me you knew things."

"Like?"

"I don't know. Maybe things other people didn't know. A different slant on things."

"Maybe I do."

"Maybe. But you don't seem to understand what's going on any better than anyone else."

"Recess, counselor," said Tyler. "You might want to consider the possibility that you may be lost somewhere in the process. You're talking about events in your life. You will always have events; some you'll call good, some bad, some in between. That's the way life is. Most drunks and addicts, most people in recovery, are event-oriented. So when we start talking about a Process, capital P, the eyes glaze over and the mind begins to wander. Hey, man, where's the event? This is Friday, where's the event? We are talking about spiritual principles. Doesn't have anything to do with events."

"But . . ."

"This could go on all night," said Tyler. "Let's get back to basics. What does chapter 57 in the Tao say about the Third Step? First three lines."

"You govern a kingdom by normal rules,
You fight a war by exceptional moves;
But you win the world by letting go."

"Letting go, eh?" said Tyler. "Interesting. Next two lines."
How do I know this is true?
By what is within me."
"Get it?" said Tyler. "Less and less," said Bob. "It's an inside job?"
"Your grade point average is going way down after tonight's class. You doing a meditation in the morning?"
"In the shower. Sometimes in my car on the way to work."
"Sounds a little too casual, counselor. Perhaps an appointment with your higher power on a more regular basis would help. Same time, same place every day. Find a place to sit and breathe in and out."
"Breathe in and out?" said Bob. "This is a spiritual thing? This breathing in and out?"
"Very. Actually, it's breathing *out* and breathing *in,* but we don't have to get into the finer points right now. If you feel adventurous, count your breaths. But don't read anything before meditation, anything you can think about while communing with your breath."
"Except my homework," said Bob. "The stuff you give me to read. I can read that."
"Not before meditation."
"Maybe I should be taking notes, so I won't forget all these important instructions."
"Not a bad idea," agreed Tyler. "Most people in recovery have very bad memories. Whether it's food, whiskey, heroin, sex or whatever, we have trouble remembering what it was like. We seem doomed to do those crazy, self-destructive things over and over until we either end up in the loony bin or are fortunate enough to die."

Tyler's voice went flat. "Go on up to the mental hospital in Camarillo and catch a meeting there sometime. Take a tour of the grounds, say hello to the guys in the Mickey Mouse suits first, check out the group at the lunch counter who are dancing to music only they can hear, then go to a meeting and watch the people twitch while you share your experience, strength and hope. A few wet brains, a few on Prolixin, some who had maybe four drinks too many one day and just signed out. Good-bye. They're gone. You're talking to cardboard cutouts; the real people left a long time ago for safer territory. I think of them sometimes when having a drink sounds like it might be a good idea. I think of Irish Jimmy doing a dance in his bare feet on all that broken glass on the kitchen floor. Jamiesons and blood. Jimmy loved to dance." Tyler paused. "Ah, never mind. I'll get off my soapbox. You read Kabir?"

"I like Kabir," said Bob.

"All is not lost. What does Kabir say about recovery?"

"If saying money made you rich
No one would be poor."

"Good," said Tyler.

"Isn't that what you always say? Talk is cheap? Action is the magic word?"

"It's one of the things I always say. I also do some biblical things, like 'Faith without works is crapola.'"

"That's the new, modern translation? Crapola?"

"The latest," said Tyler. "Here's my favorite Kabir:

"Speech is priceless
If you speak the truth.
Weigh it on the scales of the heart

Before it comes out of the mouth."

"Language of the heart," said Bob.

"Yeah."

"I knew that was your favorite when I read it."

"I certainly hope I'm not getting predictable. There goes the mystique. What did you get out of *The Varieties of Religious Experience?*"

"Not much. Mostly heavy going. Seems to be where Bill W. gets the term Higher Power. I got a few quotes. I like this one from Havelock Ellis:

"Laughter of any sort may be considered a religious exercise, for it bears witness to the soul's emancipation.

"But mostly it was a mixed bag," said Bob. "I didn't get much out of it."

"Probably not much there to get."

"So why did you have me read it?"

"Because it's part of your spiritual heritage. And now we're going to do something you'll like even less. We're going to recite the Third-Step prayer together. Kneeling down. Holding hands."

"Tyler, give me a break."

"It's on page sixty-three. Big Book's right there."

"I can't believe you want me to do this."

"Believe, Bob. Believe."

"Shouldn't we turn the tape off?"

"Why? You think people will be able to see that we're holding hands?"

"No, it's just . . . I mean this whole thing seems . . ."

"Come on," said Tyler. "And speak up so the tape will pick it up."

"Jesus."

[Shuffling of chairs, a few moments of silence, then two voices at a distance.]

"God, I offer myself to Thee—to build with me and to do with me as Thou wilt. Relieve me of the bondage of self, that I may better do Thy will. Take away my difficulties, that victory over them may bear witness to those I would help of Thy power, Thy love, and Thy way of life. May I do Thy will always."

[The scraping of chairs is followed by the two distinct voices, much closer now.]

"How do you feel?" said Tyler.

"Stupid."

"Yeah," said Tyler. "I don't blame you. There's really only one good line in the whole prayer."

"Which one's that?"

"Relieve me of the bondage of self. Actually, it's only half a line."

"If there's only one good line in it, how come we had to kneel down, hold *hands* for chrissakes, and say the whole thing?"

"To see if you were desperate enough to go on to the next step."

"I pass the desperation test?" said Bob.

"With flying colors."

"You know, it occurs to me that I never see you say the Lord's Prayer at meetings."

"True," said Tyler. "Haven't said it in maybe ten years."

"Everybody says the Lord's Prayer, Tyler."

"But me."

"But you. Why?"

"I don't say it because I think it's a horseshit prayer. You want a good prayer, read Walt Whitman. Besides, I never had any good feelings about my own father. I just don't identify with the heavenly version."

"One of these days, they're going to run you out of AA."

"Can't," said Tyler. "Read the first tradition. I get to stay no matter what."

"So," said Bob, "that's it? We done enough stupid, degrading things for one night?"

"I think so," said Tyler. "You been going to the Rusty Zipper Group?"

"Last two Thursdays. I'll be making coffee myself this week."

"Think you can handle it?"

"Mac has his doubts, but I don't see any problems. I get a chuckle out of it; they don't know who I am."

"Sure they do," said Tyler. "You're just another drunk."

"Oh. Right."

"Next time is Step Four, counselor—a searching and fearless moral inventory."

"That's me, searching and fearless."

"Read up to page seventy-one in the Big Book and the appropriate chapter in the Twelve and Twelve. Write a fear inventory and a sex inventory."

"In two weeks?" said Bob.

"Then check out chapter 33 in the Tao, and find the passage in *The House at Pooh Corner* that applies to the Fourth and Fifth Steps."

"In two weeks?"

"You just said that," Tyler pointed out. "The answer is yes. And one more thing—find out what Winnie-the-Pooh's real name is."

"Is it Bill W.?"

"No."

"Dr. Bob?"

"No, but you may be getting close. Make a small sign that says, 'Do not take thyself too seriously' and tape it to the bathroom mirror. Have it be the first thing you see every morning."

"That'll make me feel better?"

"Maybe. And it may help you establish some priorities for the day. You remember the story of Pandora's Box?"

"Sure. The gods sent this box to Pandora with strict instructions not to open it."

"Which of course she did, letting out all sorts of things that would trouble mankind forever. Only one thing was left in the box."

"I remember," said Bob. "Only hope was left."

"Only hope, so that life would be possible. Recovery's about hope, counselor."

"So that life will be possible. You mind if I ask you something?"

"You need my permission?"

"It's about your daughter. Was she drunk that night? The night she died?"

[A three-second pause.] "Yeah, she was drunk," said Tyler.

"I'm sorry." [Silence.] "Well, see you in a couple of weeks."

"It's a deal. Happy trudging, counselor."

"'Happy trudging'—Jesus."

"Bob."

"Yeah?"

"Your daughter's not going to kill herself."

"How do you know that?"

"Some things are just known."

"Hope you're right. Good night, Tyler."

Step Four

"What a week," said Bob.

"How are you on nursery rhymes?"

"You mean 'Mary Had a Little Lamb'? Stuff like that?"

"Yeah."

"I'm a little out of practice."

"You sing?" said Tyler.

"Sing what?"

"Anything. Just sing."

"I didn't prepare for a singing nursery-rhyme quiz."

"Well, you don't actually have to sing it. It helps, but you don't have to. The tune's a little like 'Rock-a-Bye Baby.' A little. It goes like this:

"The day that is here,
Is ever so dear,
And I really have nothing to fear."

"Except bad nursery rhymes," said Bob.

"Come on," said Tyler. "I'll start:

"The day that is here,
Is ever so dear . . ."

[A thin, reedy tenor joined the shaky baritone.]
"And I really have nothing to fear."

"Not bad," said Tyler. "A little practice and we could take it on the road."

"Where do you come up with this stuff?"

"This one just came to me. Standing in front of the mirror one day during one of those awful, dark days, nothing going right; just standing there and I heard it."

"On the radio?"

"No, in my head."

"Like voices?"

"Voices and music," said Tyler.

"I mean you didn't get any instructions to go with it? Like tips on the races? Go liberate France from the English? The location of the lost continent of Atlantis?"

"No. I sang the same verse over and over till the tears were running down my face. Weirdest thing—something happened that day."

"What?"

"Something very important. I learned how to cry. I don't think I ever knew. Five, six years into recovery and I finally learned. It was a gift. I don't think I even cried as a child. All I remember was being afraid. For maybe the first time in my life I got in touch with something inside and it made me cry."

"What was it?"

"I'm not sure. Today I think of it as something very sad, but I don't know if it has a name. You ever feel sad? Really sad?"

"I don't know," said Bob. "Sad." He thought a moment. "I'm angry sometimes. But I don't know about sad."

"Here's a passage from *Winnie-the-Pooh*. He's talking to Eeyore the donkey:

"How are you?' said Pooh.

'Not very how,' said Eeyore. 'I don't seem to have felt at all how for a long time.'"

"Meaning . . . ?" said Bob.

"It takes a while before we have a clue about how we really feel. We've been hiding that information from ourselves for a long time."

"Huh."

"You get that sign up on the bathroom mirror yet?" asked Tyler. "The 'Do not take thyself too seriously'?"

"Just yesterday. I haven't noticed any difference yet."

"What'd you expect?" said Tyler.

"I don't know. Something. You're the one who told me to put it up. What am I supposed to expect?"

"It's supposed to help you lighten up; get out of the heavy-does-it business."

"Well, it's not working."

"Give it time, counselor. Time. Trust me—the shell will crack. How's the Fourth Step going?"

"Don't ask."

"The rocky road to recovery. You know next time we meet we'll be doing the Fifth Step. Need I remind you that that will entail sharing your Fourth Step. Which, of course, you will have finished by then."

'gling a bit."

...u why is that?"

"Well . . . I mean I've *done* this before, Tyler. The Fourth Step."

"So?"

"So I've *done* it already."

"What's that supposed to mean? So you've done it before. Now you're going to do it again. Ought to be easier. You're getting down to causes and conditions this time. *Liquor was but a symptom.* Remember?"

"How can I possibly forget?" said Bob. "I'm into this stuff twenty-four hours a day."

"Good," said Tyler. "Tell me what the Big Book says about resentments."

"Resentment is the number one offender. It destroys more alcoholics than anything else. And, a life which includes deep resentment leads only to futility and unhappiness."

"Futility and unhappiness," said Tyler. "What a combination. And just what is this resentment stuff that seems to be destroying us? Webster says: 'A feeling of persistent ill will or indignant displeasure at something regarded as wrong or offensive.' And just think of all the offensive things out there. Think of all the offensive *people*, for chrissakes."

"Hundreds."

"More like thousands. They're everywhere. Notice that resentment is defined as a feeling, counselor. Don't forget that. Next time somebody ridicules feelings at a meeting, next time somebody would have you believe that it's only about God and whiskey, or God and cocaine, or God and chocolate cake, remember that the thing that destroys

more addicts and alcoholics than anything else is a *feeling*.
Feelings are our connection to earth life. Very important.
Go on."

*"In dealing with resentments we set them on paper. We
asked ourselves why we were angry."*

"What's the difference between being angry and being
resentful?" said Tyler.

"Time?"

"Explain."

"Anger becomes resentment if we hold on to it too long."

"Very good," said Tyler. "Here's what Yoda says: 'Beware of
anger, fear and aggression. The Dark Side are they. Easily
they flow, quick to join in the fight. A heavy price is paid for
the power they bring.'"

"The Dark Side, eh?"

"And how does the Big Book say we deal with
resentments?"

"Your memory going, Tyler? I just read it: *We set them on
paper.*"

"Ah, yes. It's coming back to me now. *Set them on paper.*
Which is what you're doing."

"Which is what I'm very slowly doing."

"Well, you probably work better under deadline pressure
anyway, being a lawyer and all. Because you still have your
fear inventory and your sex inventory to do. All in two weeks.
Plus some minor things."

"What minor things?"

"Minor research items," said Tyler.

"Like what?"

"All in good time, counselor."

"Tyler, I really have what you might call a full plate. Plus a trial coming up in two weeks that I absolutely have to prepare for."

"That all?" said Tyler. "I thought it might be something important."

"It *is* something important. It's my goddamn livelihood."

"No, counselor, *this* is your livelihood: your work in recovery. That other stuff is what you do to make money. Don't get the two confused. *If you take care of your number one problem, the rest of your problems will take care of themselves.* You ever hear that?"

"Don't treat me like some kind of—"

"Now: what important information did you get from the Twelve and Twelve?"

"It's Relentless Tyler on the move again, crushing the opposition as he goes. I scanned it—the Twelve and Twelve. It was the best I could do."

"Committing every word to memory thanks to your Deluxe, Reconditioned Big Brain."

"Not exactly."

"I'll help then," said Tyler. "I'll read some of the important parts. You might want to take notes. *When we suggest a fearless moral inventory, it must seem to every newcomer that more is being asked than he can do. His pride and fear beat him back every time he tries to look at himself.* Just stop me if any of this rings a bell."

"Don't bother me," said Bob. "I'm busy taking notes."

"Of course."

"And I'm not a newcomer."

"For our purposes, we'll pretend you're a newcomer. Just

pretend. *But once we have a complete willingness to take inventory, a wonderful light falls upon this foggy scene.*"

"Possibly the dawn, boss?"

"Don't get ahead of yourself. *As we persist*—take note of the word persist, counselor—*a new kind of confidence is born, and the sense of relief at finally facing ourselves is indescribable.*"

"Hallelujah," said Bob.

"And just to let a little air out of the balloon, we have this: *The primary fact we fail to recognize is our total inability to form a true partnership with another human being.*"

"You think that's true?" said Bob.

"I do."

"I've been married for eighteen years. *Something* was going on."

"You think you know your wife?"

"Of course I know my wife."

"I don't mean her bra size, or what kind of movies she likes. I mean really know her?"

"Sure."

"What's her biggest fear?"

"Oh, probably something like . . . uh . . ."

"If she had only one wish, what would it be?"

"Well, I'm not sure she actually . . ."

"Case closed," said Tyler. He resumed reading. "*Self-centered behavior blocked a partnership with any one of those about us. Of true brotherhood we had only small comprehension.*"

"I don't know if that's especially true," said Bob. "Or if even any of it's—"

"My guess is that you're carrying so much extra baggage at the moment that a real relationship is out of the question."

"Baggage like what?"

"Like fear, anger, resentment, self-pity, et cetera. Yoda says that anger and hate lead to the Dark Side."

"And if Yoda says it, it's certainly good enough for me," said Bob sarcastically. "Would he lie? A Jedi Master?"

"Look to the principle, counselor. The messenger is of little importance. You'll miss a lot of messages if you worry about who brings them. Hector the Mendicant said a lot of the same stuff in the fourteenth century. He called it something else, but it was the same thing. Hector also said that if you want to have the coffee ready for the eight o'clock meeting on Thursday, you have to plug it in."

"I *did* plug it in," Bob said indignantly. "How was I supposed to know the plug wasn't any good? And how did *you* find out about it?"

"Mac said it's been working for years. Same plug."

"You have to jiggle it. That's what Mac said. Apparently I am the only one in the entire universe who doesn't know that. 'You s'pose to jiggle it, man. See if it starts perkin'. Listen to it.' Nobody told me that. Mac looked at me like I was some kind of an idiot. I'm supposed to be a mind reader? Then of course everybody's on my case. 'Where's a coffee, man? Coffee s'pose to be done by eight. Meetin' time.' Like they're helping in case I don't know what time the meeting starts. Jesus."

"I'm glad it was a good experience," said Tyler. "It was more than I could have hoped for. Nobody's telling you what a wonderful guy you are because you showed up at the meeting.

Nobody's wowed by your credentials. No, you're actually a part of the group—Bob, the Drunk. Better yet, you're the coffee maker. And they're complaining because the coffee's not done on time. Hey, it's not your fault they didn't teach you how to make coffee at Yale. It's perfect."

"Doesn't feel perfect. Never heard so much whining and complaining in my life."

"You going back this week to make coffee?"

"Yeah."

"Then it's perfect. You're doing it because you're supposed to be doing it. It's the next thing. The Universe understands action, Bob. Doesn't make any difference whether you feel like doing it or not. You're doing it. That's what counts."

"Hector the Mendicant, eh? The fourteenth-century coffee maker."

"Father Hector was ahead of his time," said Tyler. "A true visionary."

"That reminds me," said Bob. "I met a priest the other day."

"Didn't I warn you about going to church?" said Tyler.

"No, at a meeting."

"The Rusty Zipper Group?"

"Yeah. Eddy something. Really a nice guy."

"We get only the best."

"He's looking for a sponsor."

"Do I hear opportunity knocking?"

"You think I should?"

"Are you kidding? This is like something that dropped out of the sky. A gift. Of course you should. Sit down with him first and see if he's willing to do all those stupid degrading things *you* have to do to stay sober."

"I don't really feel that way," said Bob. "At least not all the time."

"Well, that's a relief," said Tyler. "Keep me posted about Eddy. I have a hunch this will be very interesting. Now, what did you find in *The House at Pooh Corner* that relates to the Fourth and Fifth Steps?"

"Took a while, but I got it.

"Pooh began to feel a little more comfortable, because when you're a Bear of Very Little Brain and you Think of Things, you sometimes find that a thing which seemed very Thingish inside you is quite different when it gets out in the open and has other people looking at it."

"Bingo, counselor," said Tyler.

"Nailed it, eh? *Admitted to God, to ourselves and to another human being the exact nature of our wrongs.*"

"Perfecto. And very Thingish."

"We're as sick as our secrets?"

"We are indeed."

"A-plus, boss?"

"Not quite. We'll save the As for the difficult terrain up ahead."

"You're tough, Tyler."

"I'll take that as a compliment. Chapter 33 of the Tao?"

"He who knows men is clever.

He who knows himself has insight."

"The Big Book says that by this time we have probably managed to swallow and digest some big hunks of truth about ourselves."

"'He who knows himself has insight,'" said Bob.

"Sometimes that's true," said Tyler.

"Only sometimes?"

"No guarantees, counselor."

"No? I'm trying to find some solid ground here, Tyler, some place to stand, and here you are all over the map."

"If you're looking for guarantees, you're looking in the wrong place. You want safety, solid ground, buy more insurance or build a bomb shelter. You want Life, open the door and take your chances. You want a gold ring, get on board. Life is beckoning, counselor. The illusion of safety is like the illusion of control—all smoke and mirrors. No such thing. Were I a religious person, I would say that you will have to learn to have faith, faith in the Process. Since I'm not, I'll suggest that you learn to trust. Day at a time. Hour at a time. Trust. Open the door and trust. A spiritual path doesn't offer safety, it offers Life. Not the same thing. Remember it's a journey. And at some level you've already arrived at your destination."

"Already arrived, eh?" said Bob. "This going to be another one of those sound-of-one-hand-clapping things?"

"Here's what Thomas Merton says. This is from *Reflections on Prayer*.

"You start where you are and you realize that you're already there. We already have everything, but we don't know it and we don't experience it."

"That certainly clears everything up," said Bob dryly. "And if it's true that I'm already there, why don't I feel like it?"

"Because, counselor, the awareness that you're already there is hidden under a lot of excess baggage and a really lousy belief system. Turns out you got a lot of bad information as you were growing up."

"We getting down to causes and conditions now?"

"We're starting," said Tyler. "That's one piece of the puzzle. Just one. Others will be revealed as we go along."

"To arrive at a place we already are. Or are already. Take your pick."

"You remember this?" said Tyler.

"When it's cold,
When it freezes,
I'll be safe,
In the arms of Jesus."

"No," said Bob. "Must be Protestant."

"I doubt it. My mother used to say it all the time. She was big on novenas, too. St. Jude, Patron Saint of Hopeless Causes. She made a novena to St. Jude once a month for my father. First nine days of the month. Every month. But my father was a little too tough even for old St. Jude. Whiskey ate his liver before St. Jude could get to him."

"Everybody's busy these days."

"Yeah. The point is that recovery isn't about safety or solid ground. Recovery is about a journey through the dark part of the forest, about tears and heartbreak and an incredible sense of joy, about learning how to be a child, about opening the door that lets Life in, about freedom from alcohol, drugs, addictions of all kinds. It's about action, about doing things, not *thinking* things. Recovery is Life, counselor. Life itself. Up close and personal. And sometimes, during those up-close-and-personal encounters, Life seems to be wearing a sandpaper suit. Not to worry—it's just to smooth out a few of the rough spots."

"On the journey to the place we already are," said Bob.

"Now you're getting it."

"Of course. By the way, Winnie-the-Pooh's real name is Edward Bear."

"You're a pistol," said Tyler. "Okay. Finish up your inventories for next time. Do the usual lessons in the Big Book and the Twelve and Twelve. Find the verse in *Alice in Wonderland* that best describes the journey." [A groan from Bob.] "Only one more," said Tyler. "Get a book of poetry by Rumi."

"Spell, please."

"R-u-m-i. Find the verse that applies to the Fifth Step. Hint," said Tyler. "Try the quatrains."

"Let it be noted that I am leaving before you come up with anything else."

"So noted, counselor. You have to be out of the house when—next week?"

"By Friday. I have secured a small, shabby apartment over on Tularosa."

"In the Land of Nod? To the east of Eden?"

"Very biblical, Tyler. Though a little out of character for you. It's seven-forty-seven Tularosa. I'll have a phone by the weekend."

"Good. How is your daughter?"

"Donna is treading a narrow path, but okay at the moment."

"Like her dad," said Tyler.

"Maybe."

"And maybe you're both growing up at the same time."

"Good night, Tyler."

"Good night, Bob. Happy trudging. Remember that I love you. That's important."

"Jesus H. Christ, Tyler. You make me crazy, you know that?"

"Good night."

Step Five

"Nice place," said Tyler. "Little tough to find, though."

"Three hundred a month doesn't get you very far uptown."

"Where's the furniture?"

"You're looking at it."

"Kitchen table and two chairs?"

"Don't forget the fridge and the stove."

"Those are appliances, not furniture," said Tyler. "Probably wasn't much trouble to move, eh?"

"Couple of trips for clothes and that was about it. Five years sober and I've got an old suitcase and some clothes."

"Always helps to travel light. No bed?"

"Comes next week," said Bob. "Along with the rest of the stuff from Abby Rents. For now I'm sleeping on the floor in the sleeping bag."

"Sleeping on the floor's supposed to be good for your back."

"Back problems are way down on my list of problems."

"Home sweet home. What would Abby Rents do without addicts and alcoholics? Seems almost monastic, counselor. Perhaps an appropriate setting for your journey."

"The significance escapes me at the moment."

"Bare bones," said Tyler. "Down to the metal. No excess baggage."

"Bottom of the barrel? Nowhere to go but up?"

"That's the theory," said Tyler. "You ready for the Fifth Step?"

"Ready as I'll ever be."

"Is that thick notebook there filled with atrocities dredged from the nightmare past of your drinking and drugging days?"

"Inventories for every occasion," said Bob. "Long ones, short ones, ones about fear, about sex, something for everyone. Step right up and . . . "

"You take a look at the Big Book and the Twelve and Twelve?"

"I did."

"And what did it say about the Fifth Step?"

"If we skip this vital step, we may not overcome drinking."

"You believe that?" said Tyler.

"I'm not sure. What I think is that I'm willing to believe."

"Good. Also says somewhere in there that the practice of admitting one's faults to another person is part of an ancient tradition."

"I'm not interested."

"It's history."

"Maybe. Or maybe it's horseshit, Tyler."

"Then why are you doing it?"

"Because it's the next thing. It's in front of me. I'm Bill W.'s version of Pavlov's dog."

"I like that," said Tyler. "What other gems did your reading provide?"

"Something to the effect that we often try to convince ourselves that certain humiliating experiences are best kept secret."

"True. I'm as sick as my secrets. Don't tell anyone about the whipped cream and the banana."

"What?"

"Never mind," said Tyler. "Continue."

"You believe alcoholics are tortured by loneliness?" asked Bob. "It says that in the Twelve and Twelve."

"I could believe that. Right after that comes one of my favorite lines:

"It was as if we were actors on a stage suddenly realizing that we did not know a single line of our parts."

"And why is it we don't know any of the lines, boss?"

"No script," said Tyler. "We've been winging it for so long, we don't have a clue about what our part really is. And of course asking is out of the question. Someone might discover that we don't know everything. Or anything. We're life's chameleons, counselor, adapting to our surroundings with lightning speed, finding the required role, picking up the lingo, the body language—emotional quick-change artists.

"What do you want me to be today?" Tyler continued. "Just name it. You want the Intellectual? That's me. The

Tough Guy? Mr. Blue Collar? No problem. I can do a role a day. Easy. A role an hour. I'm a survivor, man. This is life's road show and I'm on the road. But if you want to know who I really am, what my part is, what my lines are, you're out of luck. I don't have a clue."

"The actor again," said Bob. "Moving the lights, the scenery, the players. If only people would do what we wanted, everything would be okay."

"You've actually been reading the book."

"Surprised?"

"Stunned," said Tyler.

"Ye of little faith."

"Guilty as charged. Sometimes I underestimate people."

"Bad habit."

"Agreed," said Tyler. "And not my only character defect."

"How many of these inventories have you done?" said Bob.

"Just the one. I did some belief inventories later on."

"How come just one? I know people who do them every year."

"We can discuss that when we get to the Tenth Step."

"Someone told me your sponsor died when you were fairly new."

"True. Long time ago."

"They said he was drinking."

"Died drunk in the County Hospital. Some anonymous white room, tied to the bed, raging about life, chewing on his tongue. Drank when he was about five years sober and never got back. Tried, but it just didn't work. Too many roadblocks. If I know Fred, he tried real hard. Guess it just wasn't in the cards."

"You ever get another sponsor?"

"No."

"Why?" said Bob.

"I thought I was supposed to be the one asking the questions."

"You said it was a two-way street."

"Have to be more careful about what I say," said Tyler. "The answer to the question is, I don't know."

"Come on, Tyler. You know."

"Well . . . mostly stubborn, I guess. That more than anything. I wanted to do it my way. I don't recommend it."

"Book says that going it alone in spiritual matters is dangerous."

"Book's right," said Tyler.

"You made it."

"I didn't say it was impossible; just dangerous. No need to have everyone be stupid and arrogant. It helps to have someone point out the obvious hazards. 'Downhill: Trucks Use Low Gears—Winding Road.' The signs are everywhere. That's the good news. Bad news is that we often can't see them."

"Hidden?"

"Worse. They're out in plain sight."

"Then why can't we see them?" said Bob.

"I think it's because we're looking for something else."

"Like what?"

"I'm not sure. But one day you'll see a sign that says, 'It's an Inside Job,' or 'You're a Child of the Universe,' and you'll know that the sign has always been there, that the information is true and has always been available to you, but somehow you couldn't see it till you got to a certain place in your life. A certain time. It's one of those you-can't-see-it-till-you-see-it-deals. But it's always been there. Always."

"We were looking for something else?"

"Maybe we were looking for signs that said, 'People Are No Damn Good,' or 'Life Is Really Tough.' Anything to reaffirm old beliefs that help keep us sick and crazy."

"Thirty miles of bad road."

"At least thirty," said Tyler. "Add to that the tunnel vision that most of us have and you come up with a very limited view of life."

"It's a wonder any of us make it."

"It is. Somewhere in the literature it says that Step Five is the beginning of true kinship with man and God."

"In that order?" said Bob.

"Probably. You ready?"

"Ready or not, here we come."

"Time to stand and be counted," said Tyler. "No place to run and no place to hide."

"We're not going to leave the tape recorder running through this, are we?"

"No. This is just between you and me."

"And God," said Bob.

"Maybe."

"Maybe? How can you say maybe?"

"Easy. Listen: may-be."

"You're making me crazy again, Tyler. I'm looking for something to hang on to, to believe in. Even God. My absolute last resort. And you come up with this maybe crap. I can't do any more maybes. If this doesn't work, I don't know what I'll do. I mean, there *isn't* anything else. And I'm not going to go around feeling like this for the rest of my life. I'm . . . afraid."

"Afraid," said Tyler. "I like the sound of that."

"Jesus H. Christ."

"It has a certain authentic ring to it."

"How can you like the fact that I'm afraid? Or that I'm going crazy?"

"I didn't say I liked it."

"You just said it. Just now."

"I said I liked the *sound* of it," said Tyler. "There are some things that you cannot possibly know yet. It's not time. And one of those things has to do with losing your mind to find it."

"Tyler . . ."

"Don't underestimate the power of despair, counselor. If you are true to the process, true to yourself, and keep moving through it no matter how bad it hurts or how frightening it gets, you will eventually reach a place where you will understand that it has all been worth it."

"Eventually," said Bob.

"Eventually. The pain will diminish and you will realize that you hold in your hand the Pearl of Great Price."

"I have to lose my mind to get it? This Pearl of Great Price? You sure this isn't the old dinosaur turd trick again?"

"Big brains don't work in the spiritual life," said Tyler. "You know that. They're actually a handicap. Stop trying to figure it out."

"Yes, master."

"There's a Native American story about the fierce old Hog Woman who stands at the gate to the Afterlife. If you have scars when you get there, she lets you in. If you don't, she plucks out your eyes and you wander around blind for all eternity. The lucky ones have scars."

"The warriors, eh?" said Bob. "Well, I shouldn't have to worry; seems like I'm getting my share of scars."

"Bodes well for your sight in the Afterlife," said Tyler. "And remember that I honor you, counselor. You and your journey. The things that I do, that I say, are things that seem to be, at least to me, things that will speed you on your way. Sometimes they may not be. But I love you enough to tell you the truth as I see it. If you seem to be drifting toward a cliff, I will tell you that. If you seem to be resisting because resisting is what you've always done, I will tell you how dangerous that might be."

"Shut that thing off," said Bob. "The tape. Let's get started."

"Hope this doesn't take too long," said Tyler. "I have to go bowling at nine."

"Tyler . . ."

"Just kidding, counselor."

Click!

❋　❋　❋

Click!

"You turn the tape back on?" Bob sounded pensive, a little dazed.

"Just now."

"Well, what do you think?"

"I only have one test," said Tyler. "Did it come from the heart?"

"And?"

"And yours obviously did. Thank you for trusting me enough to share it. How do you feel?"

"I'm not sure."

"Just reach in and grab a feeling, counselor. Any feeling."

"Confused. A little guilty maybe, like I've done something wrong, revealed too much. Afraid that if people find out what I'm really like, it'll be all over."

"The fatal flaw," said Tyler. "How would they find out?"

"Well, *you* know."

"And what I know shall return to the grave with me. You know that."

"I hope."

"Be assured that I have no desire to spread these unsavory tales around. It might reflect badly on me. I can hardly afford that. You know how important looking good is. And of course, now you know things about me that are certainly less than flattering."

"That's right, I do," said Bob. "You really do those things to your neighbor's pig?"

"You don't think I could make up something like that, do you? And just as a point of reference, I don't see it as one of my finest moments."

"And some of those other things you did after you got sober, eh?"

"Yeah," said Tyler. "Some long after."

"It's a wonder you're still sober."

"It is," agreed Tyler. "Though you may be in for a shock if

you think that long-term recovery automatically leads to a place where there are no problems, where life presents a panoramic view of endless blue skies and smooth roads. Not so. At least if your life is anything like mine."

"Well, what *does* the view look like from thirty years into the process?"

"It looks like a grand experiment, one that I probably took far too seriously when I was younger. It now looks like play, something most addicts and alcoholics don't know anything about. Like it's supposed to be fun, the whole thing. What a concept—fun. Edgar Cayce probably had it right: 'You just keep coming back till you get it right.' Like the program. Nothing to figure out, gang. It's not a puzzle; it's just life."

"Sounds simple."

"It *is* simple."

"Can't be *that* simple."

"Don't get simple mixed up with easy," warned Tyler. "So. That lengthy catharsis leaves us only a little time to conclude our business. How about a quick update. Father Eddy doing okay?"

"He's having Third-Step problems."

"Tell him to go back to the Second Step. No—*suggest* that he go back to the Second Step."

"Okay."

"Step Two says all you need is an open mind. Eddy have an open mind?"

"You kidding? He's a priest, Tyler. A Jesuit."

"Tell him the key to the Third Step is willingness."

"Eddy's a ver-ry smart guy."

"Too bad. Unfortunately, we lose a lot of the ver-ry smart ones."

"What else can I tell him?"

"Just lean on the willingness part. The thing about the open mind will be so alien to him he'll never get it."

"He's willing enough. It's just that he thinks he knows it already."

"That's called arrogance."

"Can I tell him you said that?"

"Eddy doesn't have the slightest idea who I am."

"Everybody knows who you are, Tyler. Believe me. Besides, Eddy's been in AA before. Couple years ago."

"A temporary member of our research group hopefully discovering that his way doesn't work. You can help him with that, counselor. Suggest that if his way really worked he might be saying High Mass at St. John's instead of meeting with a bunch of winos every Thursday night in a room where the smell of unwashed bodies and stale urine is much stronger than the sweet smell of sacramental wine and incense that he probably remembers from better days."

"I'll tell him. Remind him."

"Good. Might save his life. Now: *Alice in Wonderland?*"

"You wanted the part that best describes the journey."

"The verse," said Tyler.

"Right. The verse. This was a tough one."

"The lessons at Life School are not meant to be easy. Or hard, for that matter. They are meant to be learned."

"Is it in the Lobster Quadrille?"

"Might be."

"To tell the truth, Tyler, I didn't remember that you said *verse* that best describes the journey. I looked through the whole thing."

"And what did you come up with?"

"Page twenty-one. This is Alice:

"How the creatures order one about and make one repeat lessons, she thought. I might as well be at school."

"Not bad, counselor. Not bad at all. Here's one that's—what shall I say—that's closer to describing the journey. And it *is* in the Lobster Quadrille—last verse:

"What matters is how far we go, his scaly friend replied,
There is another shore, you know, upon the other side.
The further off from England, the nearer is to France;
Then turn not pale, beloved snail, but come and join
*   the dance.*
Will you, won't you, will you, won't you, will you join
*   the dance?*
Will you, won't you, will you, won't you, won't you join
*   the dance?"*

"I like it," said Bob. "'The further off from England, the nearer is to France.' We're on our way, eh?"

"We are," said Tyler. "On the road."

"To where? Oh, I remember: to a place we already are."

"Bravo, counselor."

"Sometimes I think you're hopeless, Tyler. Sometimes I think we're *both* hopeless."

"Might be. What did you find from our Persian poet that applies to Step Five?"

"Rumi?"

"Does the question indicate a failure to complete the assignment?"

"I actually bought the book, but never had a chance to get into it."

"I will make an exception and read it myself, but I hope this doesn't set some kind of precedent:

"A night full of talking that hurts,
My worst held-back secrets: Everything
Has to do with loving and not loving.
This night will pass.
Then we have work to do."

"Not bad."

"Not bad at all," said Tyler. "How is sweet, young Donna doing?"

"She feels we're holding her hostage, ruining her life."

"Ah, to be sixteen again. And I believe *your* birthday is next week, counselor? Your fifth?"

"Five years old," said Bob. "Short pants, skinned-up knees and a bloody nose. Your basic five-year-old."

"Don't be too hard on him; he's just beginning to learn how to play. You going to chair a meeting somewhere?"

"Hadn't planned on it."

"Why not?"

"I just don't feel good about doing it—about being five and having to struggle like this. Bums me out."

"It's not for you," said Tyler.

"What isn't?"

"The birthday. It's for the people who need to know that it's possible to struggle and stay sober. Five years, ten years, twenty. At a minimum you ought to do the Rusty Zipper Group."

"Yeah, that might be okay. I could bring a cake. Those guys love sweets."

"And they'll sing 'Happy Birthday' for you."

"You ever hear those guys sing?"

"Like angels," said Tyler. "Don't forget the candles."

"Five big ones."

"Long time between drinks."

"Yeah. Long time."

"Good. That's settled. For next time we meet, do Step Six in the Big Book and the Twelve and Twelve. Read Rumi and find something that applies. Same with the Tao. Also try *The Waste Land* by Eliot; lots of good stuff in there. And ask in your morning meditation to be led where you need to go. Ask for guidance."

"We must be approaching midterms, boss," said Bob.

"Six is halfway home."

"There going to be a midterm exam?"

"There's an exam every day," responded Tyler. "If you go to bed clean and sober, you pass. You're doing okay."

"If I'm doing okay, how come I feel so crappy?"

"Time lag."

"What's that?"

"I'll explain later. For now, just keep moving. When I leave tonight, sit down and think about what you've done so far. Is it solid? Have you given it your best shot? If so, go on to Step Six, one small paragraph in the Big Book."

"One paragraph," said Bob. "That's my kind of step."

"Don't be fooled; it's tougher than it looks. I'll be at the Rusty Zipper Group Thursday to help you celebrate."

"You think I ought to take antidepressants?" said Bob.

"Where in the world did that come from?"

"I was talking to a woman at a meeting the other day, a therapist—Connie something—and she said I seemed depressed."

"That's because you *are* depressed."

"So what do you think?"

"Not today, counselor," said Tyler. "Inconclusive evidence."

"That's no answer, Tyler."

"Actually, it *is* an answer; maybe not the one you want to hear. Here's a passage from *Illusions*. You might want to write it down. It may come in handy someday.

"There is no such thing as a problem without a gift in its hands. You seek the problems because you need the gifts."

"What are the gifts?"

"The gifts are the lessons. It's what you have to find out. It's the discovery part of the journey. Goodnight, Bob. We have surely suffered enough for one night."

"See you Thursday," said Bob.

"Happy birthday to you, happy birthday to you, happy b-i-r-r-r-r-thday dear counselor, la deda daa da daaaa."

Step Six

"You think lust is a character defect?" asked Bob.

"Could be," said Tyler. "Depends. Who is the object of all this attention?"

"You know Beverly from the Monday night Rampart meeting? Bombshell Beverly?"

"Ah," said Tyler. "Bombshell Beverly."

"A knockout," said Bob.

"I've seen her."

"Nice, eh?"

"A knockout."

"Like I said."

"And your divorce?"

"Well," said Bob, "we're just separated really. For now. We're *talking* about divorce."

"I see. Just talking."

"Discussing it. The possibility."

"Like rational adults."

"That may be stretching it a bit."

"And this Beverly is new to recovery?"

"Oh, she must have a year," said Bob. "At least."

"Six months?" said Tyler.

"Must be more than six months." [Slight pause.] "Six months? You think?"

"How about five?"

"Five? Really? How would you know?"

"It's my job, counselor. It's what I do to earn my keep."

"Huh. Am I supposed to be impressed by how much you know about all this?" Bob said dryly.

"Being impressed is optional," said Tyler. "The willingness to look at the truth isn't. Your life depends on it. As far as the question of lust goes, that's something you and your higher power are going to have to figure out. It's one of those Seven Deadly Things people are always referring to. But of course you knew that."

"Of course. And it's sins."

"What is?"

"Seven Deadly *Sins*."

"Right," said Tyler. "Even talks about lust in the Twelve and Twelve."

"It doesn't get a lot of good press anywhere," Bob agreed.

"Step Six says we were entirely willing to have God remove all these defects of character."

"It says entirely *ready*," Bob corrected.

"Okay, we'll go with ready," said Tyler.

"You just reword the steps as you go along? Something different for everyone?"

"No," said Tyler. "This is a special willingness version just for you. Big Book says that willingness is indispensable."

"The *sine qua non* of sobriety."

"Where would we be without you Latin scholars? But you're right. If action is the magic word, willingness is the fuel that primes the pump. Question is, what are you willing to do to stay sober?"

"Anything," said Bob.

"Anything?" said Tyler. "Wash cups? Sweep floors? Give up your glitzy law career and get a job pumping gas in Desert Hot Springs? Perhaps even give up your lustful designs on Bombshell Beverly?"

"What's all that got to do with staying sober?"

"Lots," said Tyler. "Didn't we just say it was about willingness?"

"Yeah, but it doesn't say anywhere that I have to give up my career or go pump gas in Desert Wherever to stay sober."

"No, it says you have to be willing to go to any lengths."

"So how far is that?" said Bob.

"You know, that's the second most asked question around the program."

"That right? What's the first?"

"First one is, How do I know if it's *my* will or God's will?"

"And the answer?"

"Easy. Same for both questions: I don't know. But I have a hunch it's an inside job, something you have to discover for yourself."

"Thirty years into recovery and you don't know?" said Bob. "What am I doing asking *you* questions?"

"If it's any consolation, I did know once. Early on, I *did* know some things. Fortunately, I'm getting dumber."

"Dumber?"

"You know: stupider. An old Chinese proverb says, 'The further one travels, the less one knows.'"

"As many miles as you've traveled, Tyler, you can't know much of anything by now."

"Here's one from the Sufis: 'When the mind weeps for what it has lost, the spirit rejoices for what it has found.' See where we're headed with this?"

"I'm almost embarrassed to say I don't have a clue."

"That may be better news than you think," said Tyler. "The Tao says, 'Drop wisdom and abandon cleverness.'"

"And embrace stupidity?" said Bob.

"Step Six, counselor, continues the emptying-out process. It means, perhaps, abandoning the clever cocktail party banter that you have cultivated through the years, giving up old ways, getting rid of excess baggage."

"So I can be lighter?"

"So you can be emptier," said Tyler.

"As in running-on-empty?"

"No. As in receptive."

"Receptive to what?"

"Listen to St. John of the Cross:

The goods of God, which are beyond all measure, can only be attained by an empty and solitary heart.

"The goods, eh?" said Bob. "By an empty and solitary heart. Grim."

"Receptive to the gifts of the spirit," said Tyler.

"Or the Great Pumpkin."

"Could be. What's your worst character defect?"

"Depends on who you talk to."

"How about you?"

"What do *I* think my worst character defect is?"

"Is there an echo in here?"

"My worst character defect is . . . that I don't really care about anybody but myself. I'm ashamed to admit it, but that's the honest-to-God truth. I mean, I don't think I even know *how*. Maybe I never learned."

"A possibility," said Tyler. "Go on."

"Go on with what?" Bob said irritably. "That's it."

"Talk about it."

"There's nothing to talk about."

"We're as sick as our secrets," said Tyler.

"Okay, I'm selfish. Period. Selfish guy. We already talked about it in the Fifth Step. Your mind going to sleep again?"

"Actually, we didn't talk about it. You mentioned it in passing. As in, 'Oh by the way, I think I'm a little selfish.' Figure a guy's worst character defect would get a little more play than that."

"Jesus. Mr. Relentless is at it again. For one thing, I don't even know if I'm capable of caring about other people, like I should. Like other people do. I don't even think I care about what happens to my daughter. Not really. Or maybe I care because the whole thing is getting inconvenient. Or because it may reflect badly on me. But I don't know if I really care. And my marriage—who knows? Divorce is . . . awkward. A bother. The truth is, I don't want to be bothered. You know the first thing I thought about after Polly said she wanted a divorce? The very first thing?"

"Sure, you thought about climbing into the sack with Bombshell Beverly," said Tyler.

"How did you know?"

"I'm one of us, remember?"

"Eighteen years of marriage and all I could think of was getting it on with the Bombshell. Jesus."

"It's a disease of self, counselor. We are, most of us, incredibly self-destructive and self-obsessed. Nothing glamorous about addiction; it's ugly right down to the fine print."

"I ever tell you about when my mother died?" said Bob.

"No."

"I was sober maybe two years. She was in a nursing home. Senile. I stopped going to see her because she didn't recognize me anymore, didn't know who I was. When I walked into the room, she'd get this awful look on her face like she was terrified, then start rolling her wheelchair away from me as fast as she could. And . . . she smelled bad. She weighed three hundred pounds and she smelled bad. My mother. I hated it that she smelled bad. I don't know if they ever bathed her. I never even asked. My own mother. I mean I just stopped going to see her. Made excuses. Too busy. Too something. Then she died."

[A long pause before Bob continued.]

"I got a phone call from the nursing home saying she was dead, and all I could think of was that it was too late. I said to the lady on the phone, 'It would've helped if you had bathed her once in a while.' Like that might've saved her life. I actually said that. But she didn't get it. How could she? Next thing I felt was relief because I wouldn't have to shell out to the nursing home every month. My mother died and I was relieved I wouldn't have to pay the nursing home anymore. I never cried. Never. And I think I loved her. At least that's what I always told myself. I mean, I *said* that—'I love you, Mom.' That's what I said. But I don't know if I did. If I ever did. How do you know, Tyler? Really know?"

"About whether you love people?"

"Yeah."

"The Buddhists have a saying: 'What is the ultimate teaching of the Buddha? You cannot know it until you know it.'"

"That's not much help," said Bob.

"Turns out that life is a very practical affair," said Tyler. "It is much more learn-by-doing than learn-by-thinking. And try to remember that the fabric of reality is being woven as you live it. As-you-live-it. Just as you are the symphony and at least partially the conductor, you are also, to some extent, the fabric and the weaver."

"Certainly doesn't feel like I'm the weaver," said Bob. "Or the conductor. Feels more like I'm on a runaway train headed for a cliff."

"Good."

"Sure, good—"

"It sometimes helps to fall back on the act-as-if position."

"Act-as-if I'm the conductor?" said Bob.

"Why not?"

"So I act-as-if and then what? I find out what it's like to be a conductor? I find out if I'm able to love people?"

"I can hear the Big Brain working all the way over here. You must know by now, counselor, that you can't apply logic and brain power to spiritual subjects. It's apples and oranges. That's one of the reasons recovery is so tough for the best and the brightest."

"Jesus."

"There are other ways," said Tyler, "though I hesitate to mention them because they require some degree of patience."

"Try me."

"Someday you'll be in touch with your feelings, in touch with your emotional life, and you will know what it means to love someone. You will discover, as the Big Book says, that the Great Reality is within. But you will not discover it standing on the sidelines trying to figure it out. You must enter the fray and take your lumps."

"And then what?"

"Then, when you discover that Great Reality, or that Great Pumpkin, you will be able to cry when you are sad, laugh when you are happy, identify other emotions and respond to them in the moment. You will begin to live life as-it-happens. Then the doors will begin to open on a spiritual dimension and you will know . . . different things. Or perhaps the same things in a different way. But you can't know any of that until you know it. That's what the Buddhists mean."

"Just tell me we're in the process of doing that now," said Bob. "Lie to me if you have to, but tell me we're getting to that place where we can know. That's what we're doing, isn't it?"

"Surrender the need to know, counselor. It doesn't serve you well."

"God, this is all so impossible. How could I have missed all this . . . whatever it is?"

"Easy," said Tyler. "Like the rest of us, you were too busy drinking and taking drugs to learn anything useful. More than likely discovering something important like the joys of solitary sex. Talk about self-absorbed. There may actually have been people trying to teach us, but we didn't get it. Didn't listen. 'No ears to hear, man. What's the next event?' Most of us have an emotional age of about twelve when we finally get into recovery. First thing we think is, 'Man, if I could just find a girl I'd be okay.' Or a job. Or whatever. Anything to fix me. Fix *me,* man. Make me okay. Stamp my ticket. And of course the women, being just as sick and crazy as we are, think exactly the same thing. A prescription for disaster."

"Beverly?" said Bob.

"Could be."

"Do other people know these things? I mean, some of them seem so basic. Like we all ought to know."

"Some do, some don't," said Tyler. "We're the lucky ones, though it doesn't always seem that way. We're the ones who got sick enough to get well. Most don't. And of the ones who do get here, to the jumping-off place, to the edge, most won't make it through the dark part of the forest."

"What happens?"

"They drink. They die. They go crazy. We've talked about it. A few atrophy in some strange limbo of recovery, unable to go forward or backward, stuck there in a time warp saying the same things over and over."

"Jesus."

"You've been around long enough to notice that Twelve-Step programs don't attract a lot of real well people. The Second Step assumes a fair amount of damage when it talks about being *restored* to sanity. Given all that, the surprise is not that more people don't make it, don't reach some kind of emotional and spiritual sobriety; the surprise is that *anybody* makes it. That's the shocker. We get cartoon characters. That's what addiction does; it creates one-dimensional people who don't know anything about living. Can't know anything."

"And here we are."

"Here we are," said Tyler. "And here's what the Twelve and Twelve says about Step Six removing our defects of character: *Step Six is AA's way of stating the best possible attitude toward making a beginning on this lifetime job.* Lifetime job, counselor. Life-time. Sad to say, all the defects won't be gone by next week. With most of them we shall have to be content with patient improvement. Introducing a brand-new concept to alcoholics and addicts—patience."

"I still smoke," said Bob.

"I noticed."

"That's probably a character defect."

"Maybe."

"I mean I really should quit. Can't be good for me."

"You'll probably quit when you decide to quit," said Tyler. "Not a day before. In the meantime, stop worrying about it. If you're going to smoke, then smoke. Be there with the cigarette and smoke it."

"You ever smoke?" said Bob.

"Smoked for forty years, twenty sober. Came a day when I knew it was time to quit."

"Was it hard?"

"Yeah, it was hard," said Tyler. "If it was easy, everybody'd probably quit. I'm not one of those who think that smoking and drinking coffee are character defects, counselor. God forbid we should get so pure and wonderful that we'll make people get rid of all their defects *before* we let them in. We may be headed in that direction already. Should always be some meetings where the smoke's so thick you can't see across the room, where you can get a real cup of coffee and a red jelly doughnut. Always need those kind of places."

"Amen," said Bob.

"By the way, your birthday meeting last week was terrific. I liked what you had to say about gratitude."

"Thanks."

"Coffee was good, too."

"I'm learning," said Bob.

"How's your alcoholic priest doing?"

"Didn't I introduce him to you?"

"Was he the big guy with the red face?" said Tyler.

"That was him."

"Sounded like he had it together."

"He's very eloquent," agreed Bob.

"You two get to the Third-Step prayer yet?"

"He says he knows a better one."

"Maybe he does," said Tyler. "But you understand, of course, that the prayer's not important; at least, not the words. What's important is his willingness to do it somebody else's way."

"I understand that," said Bob. "What should I do?"

"Beats me," said Tyler. "Run it by your Higher Power in the morning and see what you come up with."

"Tyler, sometimes you are absolutely no help. None."

"I'm not here to help you."

"I knew you were going to say that. I just knew it."

"Maybe you're getting psychic," said Tyler. "You can amaze and astound your friends by predicting the future. Did you find anything in the quatrains that applies to the Sixth Step?"

"How about this?" said Bob.

Don't give me back my old companions
No friend but you. Inside you
I rest from wanting. Don't let me
Be that selfishness again."

"I like that—character defects as old companions," Tyler said. "Very good. And now that we've identified some of those character defects, we're going to ask that they be removed. Step Seven."

"I'm following instructions to the letter," said Bob.

"Not likely," said Tyler. "You hear from your antidepressant lady lately?"

"Last week. She wanted to know if I had made a decision."

"About what?"

"About taking antidepressants. She's a therapist, Tyler. She thinks I'm bipolar. It's like being up and down a lot. A little manic depressive."

"But we don't think it's fatal? This up-and-down deal?"

"Jesus, Tyler, she's a therapist, for chrissakes. She's just trying to . . ."

"I'm merely urging caution, counselor. That's all. Extreme caution in this case. When you get up real close to it, a spiritual crisis looks just like a psychotic episode. The difficult parts of the journey contain all the elements of insanity. Just be careful. Don't try to short-circuit the process; give it a chance to work. What if we had St. John popping Prozac after a tough day at the monastery? He might have missed a lot. *We* might have missed a lot. The darkness that feels like depression may just be the sense of despair that often accompanies a spiritual journey. Don't run from it. If you keep moving through it, the darkness will lift. There isn't anything that needs to be fixed. Not now. Maybe later, but not now."

"But why do I . . ."

"Don't ask. Just accept the fact that for today there are no answers. You're exploring a world that's not connected to language as you know it. When you ask for answers, all I can say is that you need to know more of this different language. It'll come. Not to worry. We're expanding your vocabulary."

"Lasagna, spaghetti, spumoni . . ."

"Just caution, counselor. If you have not had an extensive history of depression in your previous life as a drunk, why in the world do you think that after five years into recovery you would suddenly develop a clinical depression so severe it can only be treated with drugs?"

". . . rigatoni, gelato, cannelloni . . ."

"I seem to detect a certain resistance here, a reluctance to discuss the issue. Let's wait till we get through the steps. Who knows, you may even be open to alternate views by then."

"In my defense, Tyler, let me say that I was sitting there at the meeting minding my own business when this lady approached *me*."

"I got that part," said Tyler. "But no medication until we have finished the process. We can talk then. Agreed?"

[Short pause.] "Agreed."

"Good. You find something soothing from T. S. Eliot to end the evening?"

"Eliot never wrote anything soothing," said Bob. "But I did find something nice and depressing. Seems more appropriate. This is from "The Love Song of J. Alfred Prufrock":

"We have lingered in the chambers of the sea
By sea-girls wreathed with seaweed red and brown
Till human voices wake us, and we drown."

"Oh, those human voices again," said Tyler. "What a drag. Well, you're right, that's certainly depressing. So, on to Step Seven. Do the usual reading from the standard texts. Get something that applies from Rumi, Pooh, the Tao and anybody else who addresses the issue."

"You think fear is a character defect?"

"Could be. Also could just be information."

"How about control?"

"I'm beginning to get a headache," said Tyler. "Good night, counselor. We are entering the steep part of the journey. Sleep well."

"I just got goosebumps when you said that."

"My phone works day and night," said Tyler. "Call if you need to talk. There are no heroes on the spiritual journey. Use the phone."

"I may do that. Good night."

Step Seven

"How was your Thanksgiving, counselor?" said Tyler.

"The pits. The absolute pits. For two nights I was up almost all night wrestling with some kind of . . . should we leave the tape running for this?"

"If it's too awful, we'll erase it," said Tyler.

"People will think I'm nuts."

"Continue, counselor."

"I was wrestling with some kind of . . . demons? Evil spirits maybe? I don't know. These horrible *things* just showed up."

"Ah, yes," said Tyler. "The demons have arrived. Most everyone who gets very far along the spiritual path meets up with them, or some variety. Mine were dark shapes with coal-red eyes. I called them demons because I didn't know what else to call them. Every time I closed my eyes there they were, creeping closer and closer. I was terrified. I couldn't even breathe. I had to get up and turn the lights on. Try to breathe again."

"You turn the lights on in my place and all you can see are cockroaches running for cover. Looks like a coat of paint is coming off."

"For my sister it was a big black spider on the back of her neck. It was so real she was afraid to reach back and brush it off."

"What'd she do?"

"Lived with it until the terror went away."

"But it did go away."

"Eventually."

"Eventually. We're into eventually again."

"Here's what Thomas Merton says about this part of the journey:

True prayer and true love are learned in the hour when prayer is impossible and the heart has turned to stone."

"That's right now," said Bob.

"Could be."

"Only thing he left out was the fear. The terror."

"Listen again," said Tyler. "Listen between the words:

True prayer and true love are learned in the hour when prayer is impossible and the heart has turned to stone."

"I hear it," said Bob. "But what *are* those things that show up at three in the morning? I mean, they're not really demons or evil spirits, are they?"

"Don't underestimate the power of the mind to maintain the status quo. The ego doesn't like change."

"So?"

"So when the deep interior changes begin to take place, when information begins to seep in through unofficial channels the ego has no control over, it tries to reject it. Reject. Re-ject. It fabricates things to frighten you, to make you think this whole thing was a bad idea and you'd better turn back while you can. Often it wants to revert to old, self-destructive behavior. Like drinking. Change often feels like death. That ring a bell, counselor—that last sentence?"

"This whole thing is beginning to feel like death, Tyler. I'm out of gas. This is the twentieth century, almost the twenty-first. I can't believe we're talking about demons and evil spirits."

"What is going on is no less than a war, counselor. An interior battle. A turf war for spiritual territory."

"Who's winning?" said Bob.

"Too early to tell," said Tyler. "Remember the part in *The Empire Strikes Back* when Luke and Yoda come upon this big, sinister-looking tree with a cave at the base of it?"

"Vaguely."

"Well, there they are looking down into this cave and Luke says, 'What's in there?' and Yoda replies, 'Only what you bring with you.' With me so far?"

"Close, anyway."

"Yoda says, 'The tree is strong with the dark side of the Force. Into it you must go.' When Luke starts down into the cave with his lightsaber, Yoda tells him he won't need a weapon. But Luke knows better—listen, counselor—Luke knows better and takes his lightsaber with him. There, in the dark chamber beneath the tree, he does battle with Lord Vader, cuts off the Dark Lord's head with one powerful stroke, then watches in horror as the mask falls away and he's looking at his own face. His own face."

"You seem to have a real handle on this obscurity thing. You sure you weren't a lawyer in some previous life?"

"I went to a psychic once who told me I was one of the original twelve apostles."

"You were Judas maybe?"

"No, John."

"The one Jesus loved," said Bob. "How ironic. Long way from the Great Pumpkin."

"Maybe not as far as you think," said Tyler. "But let's get back to the story. To the message. The story is about entering the dark part of the forest equipped with only old ideas. The process reinforces the premise that old ideas won't work anymore. Even good old ideas. *Especially* good old ideas. Luke's lightsaber is an old idea. Not a *bad* idea, just an old idea. He thinks it will help him, but it won't. He's entering a new dimension. The next question is, What are you taking into the forest that you think will help you? Protect you in some way?"

"My Big Brain?"

"Just when I was beginning to lose faith, you come up with exactly the right answer."

"Thank you," said Bob. "But I still don't get it about the demons."

"They are the mind's attempt, the ego's attempt, to maintain the status quo, to protect the turf it has held for the last forty-five years. It's saying, 'Turn back, this is too dangerous. See the demons and evil spirits? Turn back before it's too late.'"

"So what do I do?" said Bob.

"What you always do," said Tyler. "You fasten your seat belt and you keep moving. You bought a ticket to the end of the line, remember?"

"I feel like I'm getting dumber and dumber," said Bob. "Gets any worse I'll be selling pencils on the street corner."

"And at long last making an honest living," said Tyler. "I offer some insight from one Albert Einstein. He said, 'Imagination is more important than knowledge.' Very important statement. He also went to some trouble to try to explain to people that the sense of separation they sometimes feel is 'a kind of optical illusion of consciousness.' You remember *The Wizard of Oz*?"

"Here we go again," said Bob.

"I'll refresh your memory. The Lion, the Tin Man and the Scarecrow were on their way to Oz to see the Wizard because the Lion wanted courage, the Scarecrow wanted a brain, and the Tin Man, who had neither a heart nor a brain, wanted only a heart because, as he put it, 'Having a brain never made anybody happy.'"

"And having a heart did? Does?"

"Having a heart creates the possibility," said Tyler.

"Huh. The possibility."

"The truth is, counselor, there's nothing really wrong with brains, even Big Brains. We use them every day. We need them every day. The problem arises when Big Brains are put to work trying to solve spiritual problems. Doesn't work."

"But there is a solution."

"Indeed."

"I think I'm getting it," said Bob.

"Slowly, it would seem," said Tyler. "Why didn't you call me when things were bad on Thanksgiving?"

"I . . . I thought I could . . ."

"You thought you could do it alone. Of course. That's what we all think. Years into the process and we still can't get rid of that notion. Mr. Bulletproof. We bury lots of those. Tough guys always want to do it alone. Women, too. Prove they can do it. Surrender remains an alien concept. What's the first word in the First Step?"

"Haven't we done this before?"

"First word."

"Uh . . . we."

"Good. First word in the First Tradition?"

"We. No—our. Our common welfare."

"Good again," said Tyler. "Try to remember that when you're surrounded by things that go bump in the night. Try to remember that you're only five years old and you're embarked on a strange journey, learning a new language and trying to surrender a lot of old ideas. This is the real work of recovery. It can be very scary. It's important that you learn to reach out and ask for help. Your life depends on it. I don't happen to have God's personal night number, but I do have several others that put me in touch with people who are always available if I should need them. All I have to do is call and they will come. They will not say that I am foolish for being so frightened. They will just come and be with me. So don't forget to call."

"I won't."

"I hope not," said Tyler. "It's bad for my image if people

I'm working with go out and get loaded. Now, let's venture into the Seventh Step."

"Humbly asked Him to remove our shortcomings," quoted Bob.

"Good. Why? Why are we humbly asking that our short-comings be removed?"

"Because they're in the way," said Bob.

"Here's what the Seventh-Step prayer says: *Remove from me every single defect of character which stands in the way of my usefulness to You and to my fellows."*

"Meaning usefulness to God and to our fellows?" said Bob.

"Could be. Could be Higher Power. Even the Great Pumpkin."

"But definitely not the old God. Not old Jehovah with the thunderbolts."

"Maybe not," agreed Tyler. "And why *humbly* ask? Why not just ask?"

"Because—and you probably didn't think I'd know this—because it says in the Twelve and Twelve that, 'Without some degree of humility, we can't stay sober.'"

"Some degree," said Tyler. "This is the humility step, counselor. Step Seven. Especially tough on lawyers, doctors, people with advanced degrees of all kinds."

"Can't be just us guys," said Bob.

"Actually, that's true," said Tyler. "Call it deliberate exaggeration to make a point."

"You're forgiven."

"Did I say I was sorry?"

"No, but you're forgiven anyway."

"Moving right along," said Tyler. "Just what is this humility thing?"

"The dictionary says it's being unpretentious, free from pride or arrogance, modest even. Someone told me humility was being teachable."

"True," said Tyler. "It says somewhere in the Big Book that it takes a long, long time to learn about humility. Not just a long time—a long, *long* time."

"I can believe that."

"Also says there was never enough of what we thought we wanted."

"Which was probably everything," said Bob.

"No doubt about it," said Tyler. "Everything made the short list—alcohol, drugs, sex, food, gambling."

"I didn't gamble," said Bob.

"Anybody who drank and took drugs like you did was a gambler."

"And the food thing?" said Bob. "You think I had a problem with food?"

"*Have* a problem with food," said Tyler. "How much do you weigh?"

"Oh, two-forty-five. Two-forty-seven tops."

"Not two-fifty, eh?"

"No. Never weighed two-fifty. Never."

"That the magic number, two-fifty? 'If I ever get to two-fifty, I'll do something about my weight.' Is that what you say? And what was it three years ago? 'If I ever get over two-forty, I'll do something.'"

"Well . . ."

"Our capacity for self-deception is enormous, counselor. And remains so for a long time. What does the Tao have to say about humility?"

"I've actually lost a little weight the last few weeks," said Bob. "Three, four pounds maybe."

"The Tao, counselor."

"The Tao says: 'Humility is the root from which greatness springs.'"

"Greatness," said Tyler. "A nice touch. The Twelve and Twelve?"

"Lots of stuff," said Bob.

"Everywhere we saw failure and misery transformed by humility into priceless assets. In every case, pain had been the price of admission into a new life."

"Ah, yes. Pain. The old reliable motivator. When the pain is bad enough we either drink, use drugs, head for the cookie jar or take some positive action. Not always easy choices. What does it say about our character defects?"

"Lots more:

"The chief activator of our defects has been self-centered fear—primarily fear that we would lose something we already had, or fail to get something we absolutely, positively had to have.

"That last was a little poetic license," Bob admitted.

"But well done," said Tyler. "How about this:

"The Seventh Step is where we alter attitudes which permit us to move out of ourselves toward . . . the Great Pumpkin."

"'Altered attitudes,'" said Bob. "I've heard that before—that AA also stands for altered attitudes."

"And what are attitudes if not beliefs?" said Tyler. "A mind set, a position, a belief?"

"We're back to beliefs?" said Bob. "Back to Step Two?"

"Hey, we never left. You believe life is hard?"

"I not only believe that, Tyler, I know that."

"Careful now, counselor. Don't mistake your beliefs about reality for reality itself."

"Meaning?"

"Most things are the way they are in your life because that's what you believe. You find what you believe; the rest gets filtered out. That's the way it works."

"No, Tyler," said Bob. "Even for you, this is too much. You mean I could fly to the moon if I believed I could?"

"Big-Brain alert! Beware of a Big Brain on the loose. May be armed and dangerous." Tyler sighed. "Earth life has some limitations, counselor. Unaided interplanetary flight among them. At least for now."

"Next thing you're going to tell me is that I sabotaged my own life. I did it to myself."

"Accept some of the responsibility," said Tyler.

"God."

"You just told me you believed life was hard. You *knew* life was hard."

"Just because I believe it doesn't mean I'm causing it."

"The process is so smooth, you don't realize it's happening," said Tyler.

"Smooth," said Bob. "That's what they used to say about Johnny Walker Black Label."

"One of the great gifts of recovery is the power of choice," said Tyler. "No longer driven by all that fear, self-delusion, self-seeking and self-pity we've been reading about, we now have choices. Real choices. And what does it say in the book about our troubles?"

"That they're basically of our own making."

"I rest my case," said Tyler. "But we'll talk more about it later. I see that your eyes are beginning to glaze over. Always a bad sign."

"I'm okay," said Bob. "A little weary is all. I get weary talking to you, Tyler. Tired. You think that means something?"

"Might," said Tyler, "but I don't know what. We did the Tao, eh? How about our old friend, Rumi?"

"I like this one:

I honor those who try
To rid themselves of any lying,
Who empty the self
And have only clear being there."

"Well done, counselor. Now, what's the news from the outside world? Your outside world."

"Under strong protest by Father Eddy, we managed to get through the Third-Step prayer," said Bob.

"I hope you absolutely insisted that it be done kneeling down and holding hands."

"I did."

"Good. He may make it yet. How are you and Polly?"

"We're talking. Civil if not actually friendly."

"The Bombshell?"

"Back burner for now," said Bob.

"How far back?"

"Not so far it's not staying warm."

"I'm suggesting caution," said Tyler.

"And I'm hearing you."

"Your morning meditation?"

"Bone dry."

"You show up for it?"

"Like some stupid lemming I am there every day, body if not spirit."

"Suit up and show up," said Tyler. "The mind will follow. Trust."

"I'm in this state of confusion. Despair maybe. Nothing makes sense. Nothing."

"You may be encouraged to know that Bill W. himself was in a state of depression for twelve years. Suicidal for three of those years."

"Somehow I don't find that encouraging."

"Then I shall read a portion of a book titled *hope for the flowers*. It's about two caterpillars, Yellow and Stripe, and how they became butterflies."

"Great. Just great."

"This is Yellow, talking to a wise old caterpillar. Actually, a wise, old, *gray* caterpillar."

"Is this art imitating life?" said Bob. "Or what?"

"I'm ignoring the interruption:

"'How does one become a butterfly?' said Yellow.

'You must want to fly so much you're willing to give up being a caterpillar.'

'You mean to die?' she said.

'Yes and no. What looks like you will die, but what's really you will still live.'

'What do I do?' she asked."

"Get a new sponsor," said Bob.

Tyler ignored him. "The old caterpillar explains about the cocoon and how, even when nothing seems to be happening on the outside, a butterfly is already being formed on the inside. The last thing he says to her is: 'It just takes time.'"

"Certainly a wise caterpillar," said Bob. "This another one of those Hector the Mendicant stories you make up as you go along?"

"No. Real book, real story."

"What happens to the other worm?" said Bob. "Stripe, was it?"

"The other caterpillar, not worm," corrected Tyler. "Since this is a children's story and they mostly have happy endings, when Yellow emerges from the cocoon as a butterfly, she finds her friend Stripe, shows him how to begin the cocoon and waits for him to emerge as a butterfly."

"And the message, Tyler?"

"Not everyone is willing to go through the process," said Tyler. "Very dark and scary inside the cocoon. Can't see anything, can't imagine what's going on. No guarantees. Just somebody's word that if you go through the process, if you do certain things, someday you'll be able to fly. Big risk. You might be stuck in the cocoon for the rest of your life. Just darkness. But as far as we know, it's the only way to become a butterfly. Not everyone is willing to take the risk."

"I am," said Bob.

"I know," said Tyler. "That's why I'm here. I heard you call."

"You heard me call?"

"Let's not get into that now. We clear on the Seventh Step? We are moving out of the self toward the Great Pumpkin. Or Baby Jesus. Or whoever. We're moving out, counselor.

There is another shore, you know, upon the other side.

The further off from England, the nearer is to France."
"Here we go again," said Bob. "Look out for us."
"Another thing," said Tyler. "Remember that when we ask to have our character defects removed, we may not know what they are."
"I know what mine are," said Bob. "Greed, gossip, envy, impatience."
"We ask to have those defects removed that *stand in the way of our usefulness to Him and to our fellows.*"
"I got it, Tyler. Greed, gossip, envy. Did I say lust? Did we decide about lust?"
"The statement implies, counselor, that we may not know what those particular defects are—the ones that stand in the way of our usefulness to God and to our fellows. We just ask a Higher Power to remove them, whatever they are. So just ask, and stay out of the results business. You're not in charge anymore. Not that you ever were."
"Thank God—thank the Great Pumpkin."
"We have reading, of course. Get *hope for the flowers;* it's worth reading. You remember asking what love is? How you know if you really love somebody?"
"Yeah."
"Read *The Velveteen Rabbit* if you haven't already. Memorize it. It's about love; how you know when it's real."
"I just put it on the top of my list," said Bob.
"Next is the Eighth Step: *Made a list of all persons we had harmed and became willing to make amends to them all.*"
"There's that *willing* again," said Tyler.
"Might be a long list."
"Might," said Tyler. "Won't get any shorter by waiting."

"No. I feel like I'm trapped, Tyler. Stuck. Like I can't go forward and I can't go back."

"Maybe you're in something like a cocoon?"

"Huh. Maybe. And Tyler? I never weighed two-fifty. Never. This time last year I was two-thirty-five, maybe."

"Happy goblins, counselor."

"Two-forty, tops."

"Good night."

Step Eight

"You look a little ragged tonight, counselor," said Tyler.

"I feel a little ragged."

"I have a hunch you are nearing the bottom of your descent, the end of your free fall in recovery."

"You mean I'm not there yet? This isn't the bottom?"

"It's close," said Tyler.

"You know, there's not one area of my life that's not completely screwed up. Not one. Even driving down the street I am a lunatic. I want to run people off the road. Off *my* road. And on the rare occasions when things start to go my way, I seem to want to sabotage them. Is that possible?"

"More than just possible," said Tyler.

"I am so spaced out at work, my boss wants to know if anything's wrong. Old Hemorrhoid Harry wants to counsel me.

He thinks I'm crazy. He doesn't say that, but I know that's what he's thinking."

"He's right."

"Thanks."

"It's only temporary," said Tyler.

"We have different ideas about time," said Bob. "Temporary to me means it'll be okay before noon."

"Not quite that temporary."

"See what I mean? Then Polly and I can't manage to have a conversation without it turning into a shouting match. Donna. Money. The house. Everything. Too much old stuff. Old wounds. They won't heal."

"You ever make amends to her?"

"Sure. First time through the steps."

"You bought her some flowers, took her to dinner a couple of times and figured, 'Hey, I'm sober now; she ought to be delighted.' That how you made amends?"

"What's wrong with that?"

"Funny how unimpressed most people are when we finally get into recovery. They want to say, 'It's about time,' and we're going, 'Look! I'm clean and sober. Forty years old and I'm thinking about getting a real job. Ain't I somethin'?' We want brass bands and telegrams from people telling us how wonderful we are for going to work and getting home at a reasonable hour. People have been doing that for years— going to work, coming home at night, taking care of sick kids, all that stuff. No brass bands. No telegrams. But we're sometimes a little disappointed if we don't get all the attention we think we deserve. Truth is, we're not all that big a deal to most people."

"I have something to tell you."

"Okay."

"This is very confidential," said Bob.

"I won't dignify that with a reply," said Tyler.

"I took Beverly home the other night."

"Is there more to that sentence?"

"And she spent the night. At my place."

"Certainly didn't have to be a fortune-teller to see that one coming."

"It was obvious?"

"Inevitable," said Tyler.

"God, I feel awful. Just awful."

"Of course *now* you feel awful," said Tyler. "Now there's plenty of time for guilt and remorse. Your amends list seems to be getting longer each day."

"Jesus."

"And a nice segue into the Eighth Step—*Made a list of all persons we had harmed and became willing to make amends to them all.* There's that word *willing* again."

"You think I need to make amends?" said Bob.

"To Beverly?"

"Yeah."

"What does the literature say?" said Tyler.

"We should make an exhaustive survey of our past as it affected other people."

"Exhaustive, eh? As in thorough? And what does it say about harming other people? About what harm actually means?"

"Harm is 'causing physical, mental, emotional or spiritual damage.'"

"That should cover just about everything," said Tyler.

"I used a condom."

"I'm so relieved."

"So you think I owe her an amend?" said Bob.

"Was she harmed?"

"I don't think so."

"Were you honest with her?"

"About what?"

"Well, that answers that question. What *didn't* you tell her?"

"She didn't ask many questions," said Bob. "Maybe not any."

"And you didn't volunteer any information, like you were still married."

"Why would I tell her any of that, for chrissakes? I hardly even know her."

"I'm glad we're recording this. I'd like to be around when you play it back and hear yourself say that."

"Oh, you know what I mean," said Bob.

"Of course I do," said Tyler. "Maybe better than you realize."

"Tyler, this lady is not the homecoming queen who lived in suburbia and burned the toast once or twice after a glass of champagne. She's been around the block a few times."

"So it's okay to lie to her because she's been around the block a few times?"

"I didn't *lie* to her."

"You just didn't tell her the truth," said Tyler.

"Jesus."

"Keep in mind that she, like the rest of us, has in all likelihood suffered a fair amount of damage on her journey toward recovery. Just because she looks good, don't think that she's—"

"She looks terrific."

"Of course," said Tyler. "It's the coin of the realm, counselor. Her looks. The currency. That's how she deals with life. It's what we teach women in this country. It's how she pays for the things she needs."

"Like what?"

"Like acceptance, friendship, love, a warm body next to her to ward off the fear that comes in a hundred different ways. Underneath that beautiful exterior is probably a frightened little girl. That or a very old woman."

"Tyler."

"It's true," said Tyler. "The most beautiful woman I ever knew died before she was thirty because she believed what she was taught—that how she looked was how she was. Or *what* she was. She was too young to have breast cancer. That's what everybody said. That's what *she* said. 'Not me, Magic Man. Not me.'"

"She called you Magic Man?"

"Yeah."

"How come?"

"I liked to think it was because I was somehow special, but actually it was because I had this uncanny ability to appear and disappear like magic. Now you see him, now you don't: magic. Without warning I would suddenly vanish into thin air, only to magically reappear several days later. Or several weeks. Old unreliable."

"You were still drinking then?"

"Still at it," said Tyler. "This was years before I quit. Years.

I was never there when it counted. Never. That's what I remember; what I regret. That was the pattern. If it really counted, if you really needed me, I could be counted on to be absent. Graduations, funerals, everything."

"Tyler the Terrible."

"The doctors told her that her best chance of survival was removal of all the breast tissue. Mastectomy. It even sounded ugly. She was horrified. 'They want to cut off my boob,' is what she said. 'No, no. Just no. No surgery. No chemo, thank you very much. When I get to the Pearly Gates, I want to have everything I started out with.' The doctors tried to talk her out of it. I tried. Told her life wasn't a beauty contest, but she knew I was lying."

"No luck?"

"None," said Tyler. "Her answer was to get the Tibetan Book of the Dead and read it at night. Getting ready for the journey. You have to understand that she was very beautiful. That's what she *was*. That's the only way she knew herself."

"What happened?"

"She died. That's how it had to end. She just died. No Hollywood endings, no last-minute cures. She appeared at the Pearly Gates with her body ravaged by cancer, but undefiled by surgery. All original equipment. And of course, the Magic Man had made a quick exit a day or two before. Too much stress. No fun being around the dying. Needed a drink to sort things out. You know. Got back to the hospital the day after she died. Too little, too late. The usual. I saw the empty bed and thought, *Maybe she's gone home.* My brain obviously not working well. I asked at the nurses' station.

They looked at me like I was deranged. I still remember the look. Maybe it was hate. Her friends never forgave me."

"You make amends?" said Bob.

"Tried to. They didn't want to hear it. Like I say, this stuff is ugly right down to the fine print."

"About this Beverly thing."

"In your defense?"

"I haven't done anything that needs to be defended," said Bob.

"Go on."

"Is it possible that you're losing touch with what's going on out there? Out in the real world? I mean, sex is not that big a deal anymore. Not like it was forty years ago. It's more casual now. More natural."

"More trivial?" said Tyler.

"There's nothing in the program that says we can't get a little from time to time. Nothing that says we have to live like monks. Nothing."

"I knew I could depend on you to do the research, and cite a lack of precedent to legitimize your behavior."

"Nothing wrong with my behavior," insisted Bob. "We are two mature consenting adults."

"Well, two adults anyway. We can leave the mature for later consideration. And you're right; there's nothing says we have to live like monks. What it does say is that *if our conduct continues to harm others, we are quite sure to get drunk.* Quite sure, counselor."

"It says that in the Big Book?" said Bob.

"It does."

"How could I have missed it?"

"Possibly selective reading," said Tyler. "You remember what H.O.W. stands for?"

"Sure. Honesty, open-mindedness and willingness. The well-known essentials of recovery."

"Well, this is one of the places where honesty counts. Counts a lot. We've already talked about willingness, and open-mindedness will come up later. Here's what Bill W. says about honesty: *The deception of others is nearly always rooted in the deception of ourselves.*"

"So you think I'm deceiving myself?" said Bob.

"What did we say last time about our capacity for self-deception?" said Tyler.

"You said it, actually: that it was enormous."

"And you agreed."

"You're suggesting that I could have been more forthright with Beverly?"

"Something like that."

"I may have been very forthright," said Bob. "I may have told her absolutely everything."

"Why do I think that highly unlikely?"

"Because you're a very suspicious, untrusting person."

"No," said Tyler. "It's because if you *had* told her what was going on before you invited her home to frolic on your Abby Rents bed, you'd feel a lot better about the encounter. A lot better than you do."

"I used a condom."

"You already said that."

"I know," said Bob. "It's important, using condoms."

"Sounds like that was the only thing you did right all night."

"No, it was not the only thing I did right all night," said Bob. "And am I to believe that you were always Mr. Honesty, that you poured out your entire life story before inviting some young innocent to share your bed?"

"No, I wasn't always so honest—wasn't usually very honest at all. But that's how I learned. Making lots of amends eventually taught me not to do those things anymore. I'm trying to spare you some grief, though it seems that may not be possible. Trial and error, counselor. You ever hear that—'God's will for me is trial and error'? It's how we learn."

"Trial and error. Sticks and stones. Jesus."

"I ruined several marriages because I had lots of trouble with honesty. And I was in recovery a long time before I had any women friends. Women I could just talk to without my usual agenda. I always saw them as something else. As someone to stamp my ticket. Make me feel okay. Validate me. 'I must be okay, Mary Ann just spent the night with me.' That kind of stuff."

"I don't have any women friends."

"Surprise, surprise," said Tyler. "Food for thought, counselor. Now, it says somewhere in the stuff you read last week that *The Eighth Step is the beginning of the end of our isolation from our fellows and from God. In the Eighth Step we begin the action that ends the isolation. We begin.*"

[Slight murmur from Bob. Then Tyler continued.]

"What does the Tao say? 'The journey of a thousand leagues begins with the first step.' In this case it's the Eighth Step. And in Step Nine we actually begin to reach out and make the amends. It's the beginning of healing. More action. 'Faith without works is dead.' I know you've heard that. We are now starting to take the process of recovery out of the meeting rooms, away from that close, protective environment, out into the world to test it. Will it really work? We are out in the highways and the byways now, or will be during the next step. Ending the isolation."

"I don't think I'm ready," said Bob.

"Another side issue. Besides, if you wait till you're ready, you'll never do it. You make the list?"

"I did."

"Long list?"

"Long enough," said Bob.

"You ask for strength and direction?"

"I did. And the Great Pumpkin sent Beverly. I love the Great Pumpkin."

"No wonder," said Tyler. "Can I tell you something about women and love?"

"Can I stop you?"

"Of course not. You have to learn to love other men before you can possibly love a woman."

"And just why is that?"

"Just seems to be one of those universal laws. Like gravity. Like you have to learn to live by yourself before you can live with anyone else. It has something to do with surrender."

"Everything has something to do with surrender," said Bob. "At least according to you."

"Might be true," said Tyler. "Tell me about your most spiritual experience."

"What a question."

"Your most . . . uplifting experience."

"Besides Beverly?"

"I was involved with a woman once who said the most spiritual thing she ever did was make love."

"Lucky Tyler. What happened?"

"She made love to everyone. Indiscriminately and all the time. I found it difficult to deal with, spiritual or not."

"Your fragile ego get bruised?"

"Crushed," said Tyler.

"Trial and error, boss," said Bob.

"Trial and error. Right. Your most spiritual experience, counselor. Besides Beverly."

"Hard question."

"We are now into upper-level courses," said Tyler. "There aren't any more easy questions."

"You know, it's weird," said Bob, "now that I think about it. That uplifting experience? It happened in a baseball game. Sophomore year at Yale. Bottom of the eleventh and I hit one out against Harvard. Solo home run to win the game."

"Long before success and prosperity," said Tyler.

"I've relived that moment a thousand times. At least a thousand. I can still see it—the ball sailing out over the left-field fence, the fans cheering, me jogging around the bases."

"Describe the feeling."

"An incredible sense of . . . something that filled me, made me bigger than I was. Some power that I can't describe. It was like I could do anything in that moment. Maybe even fly. That count as a spiritual experience?"

"Maybe," said Tyler. "Hector the Mendicant said that his most spiritual experience was the realization that he was just another monk."

"What did he think he was before he realized that he was just another monk?"

"He thought he was unique. Different."

"Nothing wrong with being unique," said Bob.

"Except that it kills drunks and addicts. Keeps us isolated. You've heard of terminal uniqueness?"

"Yeah."

"Kills people like us. Keeps us from asking for help."

"I don't want to be like everybody else," said Bob.

"That's hardly a danger," said Tyler.

"What was *your* most spiritual experience?"

"The realization that I was just another drunk."

"Jesus. You and Hector. The monk and the drunk. Thirty years in recovery and that's your most spiritual experience?" said Bob.

"For a guy like me who spent a lifetime being different, being isolated, separated from people, the idea that I was a part of something, that in some real way I actually belonged on this planet, was a very spiritual experience."

"But I don't want to be like . . ."

"Ram Dass says, 'When you give up your uniqueness, you are a part of all things. In harmony. In the Tao.'"

"I still don't want to . . ."

"Surrender uniqueness, counselor. Surrender. You have to do it before you can know it. Your fear that you will become part of the faceless rabble should you surrender to the notion that you are just another drunk is unfounded. You will, however, have to actually surrender before you can know that. Place yourself in a position of trust. You are a Child of the Universe who will be in harmony to the extent that you realize and honor your connectedness to your brothers and sisters. Last, you do not *have* a soul, you *are* a soul; a spiritual being with a body. That awareness alone will open the door to the rest of it."

"The rest of what?" said Bob.

"The rest of the Process. You remember the Process? We'll get to more of it in the last three steps."

"I don't know if I can even *get* to the last three steps, Tyler. I'm drowning. Suffocating. Every day is another day I can't face, can't get through. You don't know what it's like."

"Ah, but I do," said Tyler. "That's the beauty of it. Do it in little pieces. Hour at a time. Ten minutes. Breathe out and in. Be where you are and don't ever give up hope."

"But I don't *like* where I am," said Bob. "I hate it."

"Irrelevant, counselor. Accept it anyway."

"I can't accept something I hate. That's irrational. And stupid."

"Then you may be stuck in it for a while."

"You know I hate this whole thing, Tyler. All of it. Nothing works. Nothing. I pray. Despite what I say, I actually do pray. I ask God for help and what do I get?"

"What's in front of you?"

"Divorce. Financial ruin. You name it."

"No, I mean right now."

"Right now?" said Bob. "Today?"

"Right this very minute."

"Right now there's you and me. Talking."

"Things okay right now?"

"Sure, right now. But next week I've got to see the tax guy and the school counselor and the . . ."

"But it's always right now, counselor," said Tyler. "You know that."

"No, it's not always right now," said Bob heatedly. "Get

real. This is another one of your stupid word games. See, I can't afford to forget about next week, about the rest of my life. Guys who forget that stuff are doomed to—"

"Rumi says, 'The Sufi is the son of the present.'"

"Well, screw Rumi. And the Sufis."

"Serenity Prayer," said Tyler.

"Serenity Prayer what?" asked Bob irritably.

"Say it. Out loud."

"Jesus:

God, grant me the serenity to accept the things I cannot change, the courage to change the things I can, and the wisdom to know the difference."

"Sometimes you need to hear yourself say the things you already know. As a reminder," said Tyler quietly.

"This is all too hard, Tyler. Way too hard. I'm in over my head."

"I remember a guy saying, 'In order to experience the sunrise, you have to endure the night.'"

"Endure," said Bob. "It's like trudging. Like dying maybe."

"Just like it," said Tyler. "You remember to put yourself on the amends list?"

"No."

"You inflict any damage on yourself?"

"Considerable."

"Then you owe yourself some amends. You got the list with you?"

"Right here."

"Let me see it."

[Almost a minute and a half pass without speaking. Someone is humming "Amazing Grace" in the background.]

"Thirty-two," said Tyler. "Thirty-three counting yourself. The good news is that you don't owe amends to them all."

"I don't?"

"No. Some of them are phantom amends. Ego amends. To lots of people we were just a minor annoyance."

"How do I tell which ones are the phantom ones?"

"We talk about it, about the nature of the harm. You've heard the expression, 'No harm, no foul'?"

"Sure."

"Same principle. Pick the most difficult amend you have to make and do it before we meet next time."

"Polly?"

"You decide."

"Christmas is next week," said Bob.

"Hark the herald angels si-i-i-i-ng . . ."

"I don't like Christmas."

"You're allowed. It's one of the freedoms."

"I'll be alone," said Bob. "First time in years. Polly and Donna are going over to her folks. 'Be better if you don't come,' she said."

"No need to be alone," said Tyler. "The Salvation Army always needs food servers. The Midnight Mission has a feed. Central Office needs people."

"Ahhhhh, I don't feel like . . ."

"Just do it, counselor," said Tyler. "Take the action. Do it. Those are your brothers and sisters out there. Remember: this is the beginning of the end of our isolation. And while you're down at Central Office, pick up a pamphlet called *A Member's Eye View of Alcoholics Anonymous.* Very important. Should be required reading for everyone in recovery. You ever find the book that starts out, 'The only sin is self hatred'?"

"Not yet."

"Keep looking. Read *The Velveteen Rabbit* at least once a week. We'll talk about it soon."

"I cry at night sometimes, Tyler. When I'm alone."

"Progress," said Tyler. "I like that. When you can cry in front of people, you'll really be making progress."

"Tyler—"

"Happy holidays, counselor. Keep moving."

Step Nine

"Are we trudging the Road of Happy Destiny yet?" said Bob.

"Of course," said Tyler. "You haven't noticed?"

"I want to know what's after trudge, Tyler. That's what I want to know. Is there something like strolling or maybe skipping along the Road of Happy Destiny?"

"Just says *trudge*."

"But we don't trudge forever, do we?"

"Not forever," said Tyler.

"So when do we . . . ?"

"When is not such a good word, counselor. Especially for those of us in recovery. It is a word that relates to Time and we are trying to get out of the Time business and into the Now business. The spiritual life is a Now deal."

"A Now deal," said Bob. "I'll store that away with the Trial and Error deal."

"Listen to Rumi:

Past and future veil God from our sight;
Burn up both with fire."

"Got it," said Bob. "I am now officially into the Now."

"How was your Christmas?"

"I can't remember. I'm into the Now."

"Clever, counselor."

"My Christmas was, except for a couple of things, pretty awful."

"Start with the couple of things."

"One of them you're not going to believe," said Bob. "You know that church on Broadway, just south of Elton?"

"Our Lady of Sorrows," said Tyler. "Our Lady of *Perpetual* Sorrows."

"That's it. I stopped there the day after Christmas. Right after early Mass. I'm way in the back, last row. Only a couple of people up front. Just sitting there when I heard this voice."

"I'm sorry, but I have to leave now."

"See, I knew you wouldn't believe me."

"Just kidding," said Tyler. "Go on."

"I heard this voice that said, 'Look at the statue.'"

"And this voice didn't come from any of the people there? Someone up front maybe?"

"No."

"Okay," said Tyler. "As I recall, there are two statues up front, one on each side of the altar. The voice didn't say which one to look at?"

"No, but I knew it was the one on the right. St. Joseph, I think."

"So you looked, and what happened?"

"It moved."

"The statue moved," said Tyler.

"The hand. Almost a little wave."

"I see."

"Don't make fun of this," said Bob. "I'm serious."

"I'm not making fun. I'm waiting to hear the rest."

"The rest? That's not enough? The statue *moved*, Tyler. The *statue*. The stone statue."

"It just kept moving? Waving?"

"It went on for maybe twenty seconds. I even closed my eyes once, and when I opened them it was still waving."

"And then?" said Tyler.

"I started crying. Sat in the back row and sobbed for I don't know how long. I don't even know why I was crying. When I finally stopped and looked at the altar again, it was flooded with light. So bright I had to squint. A few seconds later the light began to fade, and the statue stopped moving."

"So," said Tyler. "What do you think?"

"I don't know," said Bob. "What I think today, right now, is that it never happened."

"I bet you don't really think that."

"I'm *trying* to think that. It seems safer."

"Maybe it was a message," said Tyler. "From the Great Pumpkin."

"About what?"

"Who can know the mind of a pumpkin? You make any amends since we talked last?"

"Just Polly."

"Good. And you were out being of service to your brothers and sisters on Christmas?"

"Food line at the Salvation Army. The Spud Man. 'Get your red-hot spuds here.' I was good."

"I knew you'd be good. Now let's get back to the statue."

"The statue is making me crazy," said Bob.

"Why?"

"I can't figure out if it really—"

"I hope we're not slipping back into this figure-it-out thing again. I thought we got rid of that sometime back in September or October."

"I know," said Bob, "but this begs for an explanation. Pleads for one."

"Not so," said Tyler. "As a matter of fact, the exact opposite is true; it begs to be left alone."

"How do you leave a moving statue alone? We are talking about supernatural intervention here."

"Made direct amends wherever possible, except . . ."

"Jesus, Tyler, you're not going to ignore this whole thing, are you? This . . ."

"This miracle?"

"Right. This miracle."

"You know who the statue really is?" said Tyler. "The one on the right side of the altar?"

"St. Joseph, I thought."

"St. Francis. St. Francis of Assisi."

"It makes a difference?" said Bob.

"You know the Prayer of St. Francis?"

"'It's better to give than to receive'? That one?"

"Close," said Tyler. "It's in the Twelve and Twelve, Eleventh Step."

"We're not to the Eleventh Step yet," said Bob.

"I'm just pointing out that it has a prominent place in recovery literature. Part of the prayer asks that we *bring light where there are shadows, harmony where there is discord.* Ninth Step stuff. Healing. It ends by saying, *It is by self-forgetting that one finds, by forgiving that one is forgiven.*"

"The disease-of-self deal," said Bob.

"Six hundred years ago and this guy knew that."

"You mind telling me where all this is going?"

"Since we can probably safely assume that St. Francis wasn't a drunk or an addict, we can also probably say that he viewed the principle of self-forgetting as a purely spiritual one," said Tyler. "Now the reason, counselor, that it applies to drunks and addicts and others of our type is that we are spiritually sick and desperately need to remember this principle."

"Most people think we're more disgusting than spiritually sick. 'Spiritually sick' is probably not the phrase that popped into Polly's mind the night I threw up on my plate in the middle of dinner at the Chez Thoa."

"The point is well taken, counselor, and duly noted. We will have more to say about it when we get to the last three steps. For now I just want to stress the fact that it's a soul sickness that most people would rather die from than admit to. Denial, counselor. You're familiar with the term?"

"Is this line of reasoning eventually going to lead us back to the Ninth Step and the moving statue?" said Bob. "That's where I'm stuck."

"It's all connected," said Tyler. "The mosaic is beginning to take shape. Look carefully. You have spent the last few months tilling the soil. Or the Soil, capital *S*. What Huxley calls the Ground of Being. Divine Ground, if you like. Now the soil is prepared and you have begun to sow the seeds of recovery. One is reconciliation. Ninth Step. Amends. Action. It takes courage to make amends. Courage is one of the things we ask for in the Serenity Prayer."

"But the statue," said Bob. "What about the statue?"

"Don't get hung up on the statue."

"It *moved*, Tyler. The statue moved. I've been back to that church every day since it happened to see if it would do it again."

"Did it?"

"No."

"You wanted to be reassured?"

"I wanted to convince myself I wasn't having a bad-statue day."

"Meaning?"

"I thought that if I could get the statue to move again, if I was paying close attention and was sure it moved, absolutely positive, it would mean that I was on the right track, that God was indeed listening and I was going to be okay. I don't know that, Tyler—if I'm going to be okay, or even if I'm going to survive."

"Trouble is," said Tyler, "if you saw the statue move, you'd be back the next day for another wave, and another, just to be sure. Then it would be twice a day. 'Stamp my ticket. Tell me I'm okay.' There's no end to it. It's not important."

"What isn't—my survival or the statue moving?"

"The statue. Moving statues are . . . let's call them psychic tricks. They don't mean anything. What you have experienced is a small crack in the cosmic egg, a little glimpse into a larger universe. In *that* universe, maybe statues move all the time. Or time as we know it doesn't exist. No big deal. You want to see a miracle, go look in the mirror. There's a real flesh-and-blood miracle right in front of you. Five years without a drink or a mind-altering drug. Check closely at the Rusty Zipper Group next time you're there. Check out any of the recovery programs and you'll see lots of miracles. Living, breathing miracles. Moving statues are a piece of cake. Routine. And besides," added Tyler, "in one of Bill W.'s letters to Jung, he said that in addition to the many spiritual experiences in the fellowship, a lot of alcoholics also reported a great variety of psychic phenomena."

"That's what the statue was—psychic phenomena?"

"Maybe."

"But I don't get the why, Tyler. Why a moving statue and why me?"

"Who knows?" said Tyler. "Maybe you were ready for it. Maybe the combination of beginning your amends and being of service broke something loose inside. That's a very powerful combination."

"You ever see statues move? Anything like that?"

"If you stay on the spiritual path long enough, you will more than likely see and hear all kinds of things. For the present I would suggest you simply honor the experience. Keep it close to your heart. It is probably wise not to tell too many people; most will not understand and instead will try to diminish your experience. Don't let them. And if you keep trudging that old Road of Happy Destiny, it's quite possible that someday you will hear the sound of one hand clapping."

"A contradiction in terms," said Bob. "Can't happen."

"May I suggest less logic and more heart," countered Tyler. "You ever hear it—this one-hand thing?"

"In thirty years, I may have heard it a few times. It might have been when someone was celebrating a year without alcohol or drugs. Perhaps when a newcomer raised his hand. Or her hand. Sometimes you can hear it in the tears of gratitude."

"But how will I know when—"

"All this will come up when we get to the Eleventh Step," said Tyler. "Let's leave it till then. Just one suggestion before we move on: stop trying to see with your eyes. Look with your heart; listen with your heart. It will give you a truer picture. It's where you will hear the sound of one hand. The kind of knowing you seek has no words, counselor. You're looking in the wrong place." [Slight murmur from Bob.] "Now, let's get back to the Ninth Step. You made your amends to Polly. How did it go?"

"I'm not sure, but I think better than last time. She still seemed reluctant to admit her part in it."

"And of course you gave her ample time to jump in and speak up."

"I did."

"But no luck?"

"Zip. It's like she still feels it's all my fault."

"This is about working our own side of the street, counselor. Just ours."

"I know, but you'd think she'd say something, give some indication that—I mean, after all, she was there, too."

"I hope you didn't burden her with this tawdry affair you're having with Beverly."

"That's over," said Bob.

"And rather quickly," said Tyler. "What happened?"

"Didn't work out."

"Can you elaborate on that?"

"She said I was selfish."

"Imagine," said Tyler. "Selfish. About what?"

"Why do you have to know everything, Tyler?"

"I don't. I'm actually incidental to the process. Closer to the truth is the fact that some things need to be known. In your case it means saying the words so you can hear them. You, not me."

"She said I was selfish in bed."

"And she didn't mean you were trying to hog all the covers."

"No. She said I was only interested in my own lousy orgasms."

"Out of the mouths of babes," said Tyler.

"She's very sick, Tyler."

"Of course she is. That's why she's in recovery. Can I safely assume you didn't tell Polly all this?"

"She actually asked and I lied."

"Good."

"Good? Mr. AA is telling me it's okay to lie?"

"Falls into the category of the greater good, counselor. If you tell her you've been unfaithful, who wins? Nobody," said Tyler. "Oh, it might make you feel better for a while, getting all that stuff off your chest, but you've certainly made her feel a lot worse. That's not allowed. The rule is that you make the amend if, and only if, it doesn't *injure them or others.*"

"'Them or others,'" repeated Bob.

"Here's what the Tao says: 'In dealing with others, know how to be kind.'"

"Bless the Tao," said Bob. "It has something for everyone, doesn't it?"

"It does," said Tyler. "And the reason we do all this?"

"So we can stay clean and sober," said Bob. "Where you been the last few months?"

"And . . . ?"

"And what?"

"You've heard it a hundred times," said Tyler. "Page seventy-seven: *Our real purpose is to fit ourselves to be of maximum service to—*"

"I remember," said Bob. "*Maximum service to the Great Pumpkin and the people around us.* Tyler, what if there isn't any Pumpkin? Any God?"

"Patience, counselor. We will soon be into the Eleventh Step. While we're thinking about ways to improve our conscious contact with God, we can decide if there even is one."

"There better be," said Bob.

"Is that a threat? Let it be for now," said Tyler. "And let me squeeze in a word or two about the amends to yourself. This is from another St. Francis—St. Francis de Sales:

"Be patient with everyone but above all with yourself. Don't be disheartened by your imperfections. There is no better way of attaining to the spiritual life than continually beginning again. How are we to be patient with our neighbor's faults if we are impatient with our own?"

"Amen," said Bob.

"You decided who your next amends victim is going to be?"

"Probably Donna."

"Good choice. But guaranteed to be another tough one. You remember the verse about children from *The Prophet?*"

"Nobody reads *The Prophet* anymore, Tyler. Not since the sixties. Sometimes you sound like a dinosaur."

"Just listen:

Your children are not your children.

They are the sons and daughters of Life's longing for itself.

They come through you but not from you. . . .

You are the bow from which your children as living arrows are sent forth. . . .

Let the bending in the archer's hand be for gladness;

For, even as He loves the arrow that flies, so He loves the bow that is stable."

"Huh. That's really good. I'd forgotten."

"Just remember that it's your side of the street that needs to be swept, counselor, not hers."

"You realize that in just six weeks this will all be over," said Bob. "We're coming up on the last three steps."

"Actually," said Tyler, "in six weeks it'll be just beginning."

"You know what I mean. Us meeting every two weeks, talking about things. Real stuff. I'll miss that."

"So will I. But I'll be around."

"You're a hard man to track down," said Bob.

"I'll show up if you need me," said Tyler. "Or somebody like me."

"Don't tell me there are more like you out there?"

"Just trust, counselor. Someone is always watching, always listening."

"Sometimes I actually believe that."

"So. Here we are on the verge of entering the heart of the program: Steps Ten, Eleven and Twelve."

"The so-called maintenance steps."

"The spiritual equivalent of meat and potatoes," said Tyler. "They will nourish and sustain you through the rest of your journey. They are the wedge that will widen the crack in the cosmic egg. To neglect any of the three is to place your long-term recovery at considerable risk."

"I'm a meat-and-potatoes guy," said Bob.

"Perfect fit. The next few sessions may take a little longer, so be prepared. Scour the literature for the cement and mortar to finish the foundation. Continue the amends, including the one to yourself."

"Tyler, about the statue. I lied about the voice, about hearing the voice."

"You did, eh? Why?"

"I thought it would make it more believable."

"But the statue did move, right?"

"Yeah, I'm sure it did. Pretty sure, anyway."

"Then I don't see what difference it makes."

"But I lied," said Bob.

"Should I call you a terrible person?" said Tyler. "That make you feel better?"

"I did it because I wanted you to believe me."

"I do believe you," said Tyler.

"But you believed me when I lied."

"True."

"So what good is it if you believe me or not?"

"None," said Tyler. "That's the point. It's what *you* believe that counts. Not what *I* believe."

"I am so lost, Tyler."

"Not as lost as you think, counselor. Wrap your arms around the darkness and embrace it; it is the home of your spiritual birth. Cherish it. The light that shines from the darkness will guide you the rest of the way."

"I think I need a drink," said Bob.

"Wait till we get through with the Steps. You might change your mind. See you in two weeks, counselor. Happy trudging."

"Yeah. Happy trudging."

Step Ten

"You just turned it on now?" said Tyler. "The tape?"

"Just now," said Bob. "I forgot."

"You realize that we have deprived our listeners of perhaps as much as several minutes of information. Perhaps even useful information."

"Not to worry," said Bob. "I'll recap the dialogue for our eager listeners. I said I wanted to jump off a very tall building and end it all before it got any worse and you said great, you're right on schedule, and I accused you of being insensitive and old and overbearing and . . . overbearing? That what I said?"

"Your exact word," said Tyler.

"Overbearing and completely out of touch," Bob resumed, "and you countered with some self-serving remark about the bottom of the pond always being muddy and some stupid

reference to *Pilgrim's Progress* and the Slough of Despond.
Jesus, Tyler, the Slough of Despond?"

"Then *I* said, 'What was it that Christopher Robin said to
Pooh?'"

"And I said, 'Was it to keep coming back? Let go and let
God? It's always muddy at the bottom of the pond?'"

"No," said Tyler. "It was, 'Hush! we're just coming to
another dangerous place.'"

"Right," said Bob. "And that's when I turned the tape on.
So here's my next question: *another* dangerous place?"

"Yes, counselor, another dangerous place. But we are, in
fact, nearing the end of the darkness, if not the danger. Being
an alcoholic or an addict means always being at risk, in some
sort of danger. The price of freedom is vigilance; somebody
very famous said that. For us, to drink or use is to die. As it
says in the Big Book, *We are not cured of alcoholism; what
we have is a daily reprieve.* Based on what?"

"The maintenance of our spiritual condition?"

"Well done," said Tyler. "Now: you have shown great
courage thus far. What will be required of you in the next few
weeks and beyond is even greater courage—the courage of
your convictions. You have arrived drug- and alcohol-free at
Step Ten. No mood- or mind-altering chemicals have
entered your system, and only once, perhaps twice, have you
succumbed to some kind of glandular frenzy by bedding the
beautiful Bombshell Beverly. All in all, not a bad record."

"Jury still out on antidepressants?" said Bob.

"You tell me."

"No advice?"

"Experience, strength and hope. What's to be gained?"

"What if I really *am* depressed?" said Bob. "I mean, what if I *do* have some kind of chemical imbalance? Screwed-up brain chemistry?"

"This another bad-chemistry day?" said Tyler. "Is it like that bad-statue day you had a few weeks back? Perhaps there's another option. Consider the possibility that you might be able to alter brain chemistry from the inside."

"From the inside?"

"Here's something from the Sixth Patriarch of Zen: 'In the beginner's mind there are many possibilities; in the expert's there are few.'"

"Stay a beginner?" said Bob.

"Sounds right."

"So I'll have more options?"

"Uh-huh."

"I probably don't have a choice anyway," said Bob. "I mean about staying a beginner."

"Probably not," agreed Tyler. "You ever wonder what would have happened if St. Paul had been on Prozac? Or Judas? You ever wonder about that?"

"Actually, no."

"Here's St. Paul on the road to Damascus when *bam!* The white light hits, he's knocked to the ground and has this vision of Jesus. Changes everything. Changes the course of Western civilization. You think that would've happened if he'd been on Prozac?"

"Tyler, where do you get these strange—"

"Or Judas," continued Tyler. "Judas is so laid back he doesn't even *care* about the thirty pieces of silver. He has doubled the dose because he figures if *one* made him feel good, *two* should make him feel terrific. He is in a Zone, and history is forced to find somebody who is not taking antidepressants to deliver Jesus to the Romans."

"I don't understand what this lesson in religious history has to do with antidepressants. Or alcoholism."

"Just making a point."

"Which is what—the road to Damascus is like the Road of Happy Destiny?"

"The point is," said Tyler, "that the drama we see played out against the backdrop of time and history is first of all an internal drama. Remember that life works from the inside out, not the other way around. That's one of the things recovery teaches us."

"It does?"

"Let me rephrase that. It's one of the things recovery is teaching us. Doesn't happen all at once. Now, if the drama is first of all internal, then we should exercise caution, lots of caution, when we tamper with our interior lives."

"As in taking antidepressants," said Bob.

"Exactly. One last comment before we leave the subject. For good, I hope. Some people in recovery can benefit from medication. Some need medication. That's a given. I don't want to discourage those people. But I worry lest we become a modern-day version of the Brave New World, a society of people ingesting pills to make us feel better. Or feel something other than what we're feeling at the moment. That's a very slippery place. The journey in recovery is sometimes dark. That's part of the process, because it is in that darkness—precisely because it *is* dark, and the intellect can't see in the dark—that all of life's important lessons are learned.

All of them. And they all have something to do with surrender and trust."

"And the lessons just keep coming, eh?"

"In varying degrees of intensity," replied Tyler. "At present it would appear that you are getting the Industrial-Strength Lessons. Seems appropriate for your age. And right, the lessons *do* just keep coming until we learn them. Then we get new lessons. And when you have learned all the lessons you need to learn at this level, they will place you gently in the ground, pile a bit of earth upon your body, and you will be off to the next level for guess what?"

"More lessons?"

"Bingo."

"Ugh."

"These are lessons, counselor, not punishments."

"Feels more like punishment."

"That's because you take it much too seriously," said Tyler. "What is it the Germans say—'time is the great doctor'? Or 'give Time time'?"

"How about, 'It's Miller time'?"

"Not at the moment," said Tyler. "The message for now is, 'No need to learn all the lessons at once.'"

"I'll keep that in mind."

"What does Step Ten advise us to do?"

"To continue to take personal inventory and when we are wrong, promptly admit it."

"Notice it doesn't say *if* we are wrong; it says *when*."

"I noticed that," said Bob. "And I know that killer line from the Twelve and Twelve."

"Let's hear it."

*"All of us, to some degree, are emotionally ill and fre-
quently wrong."*

"Ah, the romance of discovery," said Tyler. "Frequently
wrong. All of us. That means you and me. Any promises
come with the Tenth Step?"

"Two I can think of: *We have entered the world of the
spirit* and *By this time sanity will have returned.*"

"Sanity, eh? You think?"

"Maybe a little," said Bob. "I don't think I had much to
begin with."

"This is the step that reminds us to look for progress, not
perfection," said Tyler. "It's not about getting better."

"It's not?"

"No. It's about getting clean and sober."

"But don't we get better after we get clean and sober? Isn't
that the deal?"

"Some do and some don't," said Tyler. "You probably know
people who haven't gotten a bit better. Sober a long time and
still pretty sick people."

"Yeah."

"The trouble with thinking that we're going to get better
is that drunks and addicts can never get better *enough*. It's
always, I'll be better when I lose twenty pounds, get a job, get
the car fixed. When I make more money. When, when, when.
The list goes on. Forever. We're the When People. The If-
Only People. You'll never be good enough to please yourself.
Never. Guaranteed. When you get close to the finish line,
you'll simply move it. Forget about getting better. The
people who wrote that book understood about drunks.
Progress, not perfection."

"That's really depressing," said Bob.

"Why?"

"This is the ultimate lifetime trudge trip. Some kind of emotional brownout. Here we go plodding along the Road of Happy Destiny. Like cows, for chrissakes."

"The race is not always to the swift," said Tyler.

"But it is to the plodders? The trudgers?"

"There's a lot to be said for trudging."

"Like what?"

"The unfortunate thing is that we attract mostly ten-yard-dash people. World record holders for very short distances. The meteoric rise to wellness in recovery. A few years later they're gone. What happened?"

"They forgot about the virtues of trudge?"

"Traveling too fast, counselor. Nose-bleed speed. So busy getting better—'I'm better, I'm better, I'm better'—forgot to be where they were. Forgot to build a decent foundation. First time the Wolf comes along with a decent huff and puff, they're gone. Breakfast for the Wolf."

"Tyler, you seem to be getting farther and farther out there somewhere. What does—"

"Point number two," continued Tyler. "When people start talking about getting better, what they're really saying is that they're not much good right now, not at the moment. Certainly not okay. If they were, they wouldn't need to get better. But tomorrow, or next week for sure, they'll be up to speed and definitely better. Maybe even okay. Soon as they get a few things fixed. Trouble with that, as we all know, is that there *is* no tomorrow, as in Free Beer Tomorrow. There's just another today in which to lament our lack of perfection, our lack of okayness if you will, and wait for another tomorrow that will never come. Consequently, we are always waiting for something that will never happen, instead of doing what's in front of us and trusting that tomorrow will bring another today in which we will have the freedom and power to act. It's not about results—it's about action. Stay out of the results business; it's a very bad place to be."

"And who would know better than yours truly," said Bob.

"Progress, not perfection."

"On our way to the Celestial City through the Slough of Despond."

"The Buddhists have a saying: 'Whether going or returning, you cannot be anyplace else.'"

"I might like that if I knew what it meant."

"Bloom where you're planted," said Tyler. "Be where you are. No part of the journey is better than any other part. And all are necessary."

"Even the Slough of Despond?"

"Another version of that particular swamp is in *The Empire Strikes Back,* when Luke encounters Darth Vader in that cave under the tree. Remember that?"

"Yeah."

"Well, in *Pilgrim's Progress,* when Christian has to go through the Valley of the Shadow of Death, he learns, counselor, that he has to put away his sword and take up another weapon called prayer."

"Aha," said Bob. "The plot thickens."

"I hope not," said Tyler. "I would hope that we were edging toward the simple notion that all parts of the journey are necessary. Christian learns that the sword doesn't always work. Skywalker learns the same thing about the lightsaber. And we are learning, counselor, we are learning that the intellect is not the weapon of choice in all situations."

"The Big Brain deal," said Bob.

"Uh-huh. And since life is essentially learn-by-doing, and only to a very small degree learn-by-watching, or learn-by-reading, or learn-by-thinking, the only way we are going to learn the things we'll need to know is by being put in situations where we'll have to learn by doing. Lessons, lessons, lessons."

"So the Valley of the Shadow of Death and the Slough of Despond and the Dark Side of the Force are all necessary?"

"I love it when you just get it like that," said Tyler.

"Thank you. I think."

"But we digress. I don't know how we got this far off the track. We were talking about the Tenth Step."

"Last thing I remember was something about all of us trying to get better."

"Yes," said Tyler. "The unending search for perfection. This is also the part of the process when we stop fighting everything and everyone—even alcohol."

"The war's over?"

"It's been over. You haven't noticed?"

"I had a hunch something was going on."

"And we lost. That's the good news."

"So now what?" said Bob.

"Assuming that we know we lost and have surrendered to a Higher Authority, *we vigorously commenced this way of living.*"

"We're into action now."

"Into action. Full speed ahead." Tyler's voice grew more excited. "We begin to understand that recovery is a perfectly balanced system. You get back tenfold what you put in, and if you try to horde anything—time, money, love— it leaks out between your fingers and you end up with nothing. Or less."

"Or less?" said Bob. "That's perfect balance?"

"Perfect spiritual balance," said Tyler. "Here's what Rumi says:

What you do comes back in the same form.
God is compassionate, but if you plant
Barley, don't expect to harvest wheat."

"What goes around comes around?"

"Jailhouse karma," said Tyler. "Divine equilibrium."

"So now we have entered the world of the spirit."

"And not a moment too soon."

"It doesn't feel like I've entered the world of the spirit," said Bob.

"This is what the Third Patriarch of Zen tells us about our inability to perceive certain aspects of life. He's essentially talking about tunnel vision. This is from the Bird Sutra: 'The woodpecker looks for dead trees among the cherry blossoms in bloom.'"

"You think I'm a dead-tree kind of guy?" said Bob.

"If it's any consolation, you're not alone. It's what we all do. Most of us, anyway."

"The *Bird* Sutra?"

"I think that's it. It's the one right after the Cow Sutra."

"Jesus."

"This step contains one of the great lines in recovery literature. Actually, one of the great understatements: *Pain is the touchstone of all spiritual progress.*"

"I love this process, Tyler. Love it."

"You do?"

"I can't believe I said that. Maybe I'm getting well."

"Not beyond the realm of possibility," said Tyler. "We're approaching the center now, counselor. The still point. The world of the spirit. The place where things are empty and full at the same time. The Inexhaustible Void."

"Oh, boy. The Void."

"And what does the Tao tell us about Step Ten?" said Tyler.

"Requite injury with kindness,

Nip troubles in the bud.

"They go a little overboard with that 'Requite injury with kindness' routine," said Bob.

"You've heard it before," said Tyler.

"Turn the other cheek?"

"Similar. Try not to get this stuff mixed up with Christianity, counselor. It'll be too confusing. What does the Twelve and Twelve have to say about willingness and the Tenth Step?"

"Says we need: *a willingness to admit when the fault is ours and an equal willingness to forgive when the fault is elsewhere.*"

"There's that word again—*willingness*. Just keeps showing up. Wonder why?" said Tyler.

"Because it's very important," said Bob.

"Exactly. It's *the* most important word in the book."

"More important than the G-word?"

"Certainly is. Without willingness, you never even get to the G-word."

"Or the Great Pumpkin word. Words."

"Right."

"And don't forget about action," said Bob.

"Action is the magic word," said Tyler.

"Willingness and action. Almost sounds like following directions."

"Doesn't it, though? Next up will be Step Eleven, counselor. Do the usual research. We will have much to discuss."

"Important, eh?"

"For me, anyway," said Tyler. "But then sometimes I think it's because I tend to be crazier than most, so I need to stay a little more connected. How are you and Polly doing?"

"Better than I would have imagined. There may be something to this therapy stuff. You know when you said, 'We stopped fighting everything and everyone,' I really got it. The light went on. That's what I do with Polly—I fight with her. Over little things. The scorekeeper in my head keeps a running tally so I'll know if I'm behind. I have to be right, no matter what. Even if it doesn't make any difference, I have to be right. It's crazy."

"For people like us, it always makes a difference. Because if I'm right, I have a chance, just a chance, of being okay. I've got to grab for the chance. That's what happens when you grow up being wrong all the time."

"You know, I've never really worked the Tenth Step," said Bob. "Not really worked it. How can you work it if you're busy being right all the time?"

"Full-time job," agreed Tyler.

"And then some."

"How's Father Eddy?"

"Still doing his Fourth Step," said Bob. "Under protest. Says he knows more about confession and absolution than I'll ever know."

"He's probably right."

"Thinks it's stupid."

"Of course he does," said Tyler. "You still making coffee for the Rusty Zipper Group?"

"I am. Next week we're having elections for a new group secretary."

"Do I hear opportunity knocking again?"

"Mac's going to put my name up."

"You must be making some headway over there. Mac doesn't recommend just anybody."

"I've got some ideas about . . . things that might help the meeting."

"Great. And last, how is the lovely and charming young Donna?"

"I'm amazed. She seems to be doing really well."

"Teenagers are a lot tougher than you think. I worry more about the parents."

"Me, too."

"So prepare well, counselor. Having discovered that the map is not the territory and the menu is not the meal, we are now actually entering the territory and getting ready to have our meal. Happy trudging."

"You know, I've actually been feeling better lately," said Bob. "I'd call the last couple of weeks pretty good. Doesn't figure."

"That's how it works."

"Yeah?"

"You suit up, you show up, take a few steps and bingo: little by little your life begins to change. It's like adding two and two and getting four hundred. It would seem that Alcoholics Anonymous is much more than the sum of its parts. There's a magic factor in it somewhere that we sometimes forget to add in."

"Doesn't figure."

"True. Good night, counselor."

"Good night, Tyler."

Step Eleven

"Tell me about *The Velveteen Rabbit*," said Tyler.

"You look tired," said Bob.

"A little."

"Old age?"

"Jesus," said Tyler.

"What'd you say?"

"'Jesus'?"

"That's what *I* always say," said Bob. "I've never heard you say that."

"A few more weeks of this and they won't be able to tell us apart."

"Jesus," said Bob. "That's *really* scary."

"Let's get back to *The Velveteen Rabbit*."

"We doing the Eleventh Step?"

"I believe this is the week," said Tyler.

"Should I read it out loud?" said Bob. "The step? For the benefit of our vast listening audience?"

"You don't want to do *The Velveteen Rabbit?* That what you're saying?"

"I do, but not right now."

"Then proceed, counselor," said Tyler. "The floor is yours."

"I'll read it first:

"Sought through prayer and meditation to improve our conscious contact with God as we understood Him, praying only for knowledge of His will for us and the power to carry that out."

"That's the prescription," said Tyler. "You'll remember that just as the map is not the territory, the prescription is not the medicine."

"Of course," said Bob.

"And the medicine is . . . ?"

"The medicine is the action. Suit up and show up. Do it."

"Bravo, counselor," said Tyler. "I just knew you'd been paying attention. But go on; I didn't mean to interrupt."

"It's probably because you can't help yourself. I mean, can't help interrupting."

"True," said Tyler. "Powerless over interrupting. Can't help it."

"And I know where you get all that stuff about action. It's right out of the Big Book: *There is action and more action. Faith without works is dead.*"

"Wonder if Bill W. stole that from St. Paul," said Tyler.

"You think?"

"Maybe."

"Everybody has something to say about the Eleventh Step."

"Very popular with the spiritual crowd," said Tyler.

"You know, I've had this strange feeling lately that I'm being led to this stuff; this spiritual stuff. I'll just pick up a book and there'll be something about prayer and meditation. Right there where I open the book. Spooky."

"Funny how it works."

"And I finally found that book you asked about. The one you asked me to find that starts out, 'The only sin is self-hatred.'"

"I'm impressed."

"Just wandering around the bookstore, I picked up this book, *Das Energi,* and there it was. Not a book I would ordinarily pick up. In the Airhead section. Shirley MacLaine-type stuff. Red cover, funny title. Not for me."

"A still, small voice," said Tyler.

"Two other things in it I really liked," said Bob. "'Stamp out hesitation before it becomes fear' and 'Let go of everything you're holding onto. Now let go of everything else.'"

"The old surrender routine again," said Tyler. "Who do you think was leading you to those books?"

"Forces unknown?"

"Could be."

"You think God's trying to tell me something?"

"For someone who's not even sure he believes in God, that's quite a question."

"God's just a handy word," said Bob. "I'm still in the Undecided column. I just have trouble believing in a regular God. A church-type God—the kind, loving variety."

"Maybe you ought to expand your definition."

"I look around and say, 'Wow! This is the handiwork of a kind, loving God?'"

"What do you see when you look around?" said Tyler.

"Pain and suffering," said Bob. "Misery."

"The woodpecker is looking for dead trees again," said Tyler. "Shift your gaze a few degrees to the left and you will see joy and laughter."

"Forget the woodpecker routine," said Bob. "What I see is what I see."

"What you see is what you believe," countered Tyler. "Somebody has this to say about what we see: 'Perception is seeing the present with images formed from the past.'"

"So?"

"May I suggest that the images formed in your past distort your view of the present."

"Huh. Which leads us to, *Clear away the wreckage of the past?*"

"Very good," said Tyler.

"Jesus."

"I'm no apologist for the divine, counselor," said Tyler. "You know that. The Eleventh Step simply suggests that we improve our conscious contact with a power greater than ourselves. But we can easily substitute 'establish' for 'improve' if we have no relationship to start with."

"'Sought through prayer and meditation to *establish*,'" said Bob. "I like that."

"'Row, row, row your boat, gently down the stream . . .'"

"Willingness, right?"

"Willingness and practice, practice, practice," said Tyler.

"Do it and see what happens."

"Isn't that the results business?"

"No. *See* what happens, not *plan* what happens. Observe."

"I'm doing it," said Bob. "The Eleventh Step."

"And what's happening?"

"Something strange."

"Strange and wonderful? Or just strange."

"I don't know how wonderful, but something's going on. I seem to know things I have no way of knowing."

"For example?"

"Well, last week somebody asked me when I thought the bus strike would be over. Been going on for months now and nobody seemed to have a clue about when it would end. No end in sight—that's what the paper said. So somebody asked me when I thought it would end and I said next Monday. Yesterday. I have no idea why I said that."

"And of course the strike ended yesterday. Monday. Next stop, *Oprah*," said Tyler.

"What's it mean?"

"Just that some of the interior barriers are coming down. Your universe is expanding."

"Like the Big Bang?"

"Maybe not quite like that. Bill W. had the Big Bang variety. Maybe St. Paul. You're most likely experiencing a somewhat smaller version. More like a Little Pop."

"Does it mean that I'm getting connected to this Power?"

"Ah, questions, questions," said Tyler. "Inquiring minds want to know. But it may not really be necessary to know everything, counselor. Ever wonder what would happen if you did know everything?"

"I could go on *Jeopardy* and win thousands of dollars."

"What else?"

"I'd be in control. Safe."

"At least have the illusion of control and safety. No small thing. Trouble is, just as you can't ever have enough, you can't *know* enough, can't *be* enough, can't *do* enough. Drunks and addicts never can. There's never enough for us. The Tao says, 'Only he who knows what is enough will ever have enough.'"

"Leaves us out, eh?"

"At least for the first few years."

"Then what?" said Bob.

"Then, if we're lucky, we hit bottom sober, don't drink or do drugs or go on a lethal peanut butter binge, and begin the journey into real recovery."

"Like we're doing now?"

"Exactly," said Tyler.

"The Big Book says that one of the first fruits of prayer and meditation is a sense of emotional balance."

"That true for you?"

"Occasionally," said Bob.

"And what does it say is the big payoff for all this prayer and meditation?"

"'The greatest reward is a sense of belonging,'" said Bob.

"Not a bad combination—emotional balance and a sense of belonging. Powerful stuff. That paragraph ends with the phrase, *all will be well with us, here and hereafter.*"

"Know who that sounds like?"

"No."

"Dame Julian of Norwich."

"Dame Julian of Norwich. Let it be noted that I am scratching my head and grappling with the slippery forces of memory. . . ."

"Fourteenth century," said Bob. "Right around the time you were in high school."

"I give up. How do we know this Julian person?"

"Father Eddy."

"Of course. Who better than our reluctant newcomer to introduce us to fourteenth-century spirituality. And what does this Julian have to say that struck a chord with you?"

"Essentially the same thing it says in the Big Book: 'All shall be well. Though sin is necessary, all shall be well.'"

"You think our man of the cloth is setting himself up for a big-time fall?"

"I don't know, but I'm worried."

"Me, too," said Tyler.

"He wants me to read Meister Eckhart."

"Beware the formally educated, counselor. I offer something in a simpler vein. This is from the Second Patriarch: 'Buddhism is practice.'"

"And of course," said Bob, "all we have to do is substitute sobriety for Buddhism and we have another important message: Sobriety is practice, practice and more practice."

"I can see I'm rapidly becoming expendable in this whole process."

"Not so fast. We may want to keep you around for consultations from time to time."

"I'm overwhelmed with gratitude," said Tyler.

"You sure you're feeling okay?"

"Tough day at the office."

"What office? I thought you were retired."

"Not from life, counselor. Not yet. But you talk for a while. I'll listen. Save my energy for the big push through the Twelfth Step."

"Likely story," said Bob.

"Well, I'll mostly listen. At least for a while. You can't expect miracles."

"No?"

"Not about me being quiet."

"Okay," said Bob. "You rest while I read. Resting means don't interrupt. You want some more coffee?"

"Not now."

"Here goes," said Bob. "These two are from the Tao:
"Between Heaven and Earth
There seems to be a bellows;
It is empty, yet inexhaustible;
The more it works, the more comes out of it.
No amount of words can fathom it.
Better look for it in your heart.

"And this one:
"We make a vessel from a lump of clay.
It is the empty space within the
Vessel that makes it useful."

"Ah, yes," said Tyler. "The inexhaustible void and the empty vessel. Two of my favorites."

"And one more," said Bob. *"Few things under heaven are as instructive as the lessons of silence."*

"Was that for my benefit?" said Tyler.

"You decide."

"I can only be quiet for so long, counselor. Tired or not,

there's a minimum amount of talking I have to do."

"I understand."

"I was quiet for several minutes there."

"Well, maybe not quite that long."

"Time goes slower when I'm not talking. It's hard to judge."

"Shall I relinquish the floor?" said Bob.

"No need," said Tyler. "We're sharing the floor. What does our favorite Persian poet have to say on the subject?"

"Some very good things:

Union with the Friend means not being who you've
been,
Being instead silence: A place: A view
Where language is inside seeing."

"Nice," said Tyler. "You know, I think I will have some more coffee, counselor."

"Coming up," said Bob.

[There is the sound of a chair scraping on a hard floor. Tyler is singing "Row, Row, Row Your Boat" softly in the background.]

"Your coffee, sir," said Bob. "A guaranteed pick-me-up. Good to the last drop."

"Maxwell House and good Irish whiskey."

"Or even bad Irish whiskey."

"True," said Tyler, " . . . I love the last part of that thing you read by Rumi: 'A view where language is inside seeing.' Very tribal. You know, counselor, tribal people believe that their physical needs will always be met as long as they take care of their spiritual commitments."

"Seek ye first the kingdom of heaven?"

"Along those lines."

"Maybe a bit too biblical for me."

"But there's nothing wrong with the message," said Tyler. "Keep that in mind. You've just had trouble with a few of the messengers. The Eleventh Step is about priorities. It will lead you to what the Buddhists call *Mu*."

"As in moo cow?"

"No, as in Buddha Nature. Something to help you cross the river when the bridge is out."

"'Cross the river when the bridge is out,'" said Bob. "Almost sounds like a song."

"Doesn't it," said Tyler, and he resumed singing "Row, Row, Row Your Boat."

"You think life is but a dream?" said Bob, echoing the last line of the song.

"Oh, those heavy philosophical questions," said Tyler. "Much too late at night for those. I won't be able to sleep with all that heavy goo on my brain. They are not, what shall we say, germane, counselor. Those kind of questions. They are in the how-many-angels-can-dance-on-the-head-of-a-pin category. Irrelevant. Yoda says that the Jedi's strength flows from the Force."

"You changing the subject?"

"No. The subject is the Eleventh Step. Questions like 'Is life a dream?' or, 'Does God exist?' are just not particularly relevant."

"'Does God exist' isn't a relevant question?"

"No. The only thing we need be concerned with is, Does sobriety exist? Is there something called recovery that we can participate in? If we can say yes, the rest will fall in place.

We take certain actions without any real logical indications that those actions will do anything. We take them because we are desperate. Who cares if it's a dream or if God exists? If you're loaded all the time, if you weigh three hundred pounds and you're having your second chocolate cake for breakfast, if you just gambled away the rent money again, those things don't make any difference."

"I was thinking about—"

"You ever look around at meetings and think, *This must be the Theater of the Absurd—what a strange collection of people?*"

"I have. . . ."

"Sometimes I think that we are an absolutely mind-boggling collection of misfits," said Tyler. "Some in suits, some in biker gear, some with long black fingernails, some in tie-dyed shirts from the sixties, almost everyone with an attitude. There's a sort of divine madness about it that somehow breeds compassion and love. Doesn't make any sense. Probably never will. It just works."

"Father Eddy says we need to establish our place in the scheme of things," said Bob.

"Like where we are on the food chain?"

"He calls it the Hierarchy of Being."

"Please suggest to Eddy that he is just another drunk, and that if he waits to discover his place in the grand scheme of things before he's willing to get sober, he'll never make it."

"I'll tell him. I'm going to see him Thursday."

"Good. He probably won't listen, but it'll be good for you to tell him anyway. So, have we established that sobriety is possible? Full recovery from a *seemingly hopeless state of mind and body?*"

"I believe we have," said Bob.

"You ever read that pamphlet we talked about? *A Member's Eye View of Alcoholics Anonymous?*"

"Yeah. I liked it."

"Remember the end? The last paragraph?"

"Not word for word. But I have a feeling you have it written down somewhere in that notebook of yours."

"I do," said Tyler. "In the last paragraph he says that if people were to ask him what he had found in the sixteen years of his recovery, this is what he would say:

It seems to me that the blind do see, the lame do walk, the lepers are cleansed, the deaf hear, the dead rise, and over and over again, in the middle of the longest day or darkest night, the poor in spirit have the good news told to them."

"Not preached to them," said Bob.

"No, definitely not preached. Drunks and addicts don't do well with people who preach to them. Or at them. So we *tell* them about it."

"About Life. Capital L."

"Right," said Tyler. "And the good news: Life is possible without drugs or alcohol. Without chocolate cake for breakfast. Even love is possible."

"Even love?"

"Even love. Not zipper love. Or motel love. Real love."

"Jesus."

"Which brings us to *The Velveteen Rabbit.*"

"It does?"

"Of course. *The Velveteen Rabbit* is about love."

"I knew that," said Bob.

"I'm going to read a part of it, the middle part, the part about love and how you become real."

"My turn to listen already?"

"Right."

"Your turn to listen didn't last very long," said Bob.

"My contract calls for short, infrequent listening periods."

Tyler cleared his throat, and began to read.

"The Skin Horse had lived in the Nursery longer than any of the others. He was so old that his brown coat had bald patches . . . and most of his hairs in his tail had been pulled out. . . . He was wise, for he had seen a long succession of mechanical toys arrive . . . and by and by break their mainsprings and pass away and he knew they were toys and would never be turned into anything else. For Nursery Magic is very strange and wonderful and only those playthings that are wise, like the Skin Horse, understand about it.

'What is Real?' asked the Rabbit one day. 'Does it mean having things that buzz inside you and a stick-out handle?'

'Real isn't how you're made,' said the Skin Horse. 'It's a thing that happens to you. When a child loves you for a long, long time, not to just play with but really loves you, then you become Real.'

'Does it hurt?' said the Rabbit.

'Sometimes. . . . When you're Real you don't mind being hurt.'

'Does it happen all at once?'

'It doesn't happen all at once,' said the Skin Horse. 'You become.'"

"Listening, counselor?" said Tyler. "'You become.' Like a process."

"I'm listening," said Bob.

"'It takes a long time. That's why it doesn't happen to people who break easily or have sharp edges, or have to be carefully kept.'"

"Or to guys who are too smart," Tyler added.

"I got it," said Bob. "Put the hammer away."

"'Generally, by the time you are Real, most of your hair has been loved off, your eyes drop out and you get loose in the joints. Very shabby.'"

"Like you," said Bob. "Very shabby."

"Exactly. You know how wonderful it is to have your hair loved off? Listen to the rest:

"'But those things don't matter, because once you're Real, you can't be ugly except to people who don't understand.'

'I suppose you're Real?' said the Rabbit, then wished he hadn't said it because he thought the Skin Horse might be sensitive.

'The Boy's Uncle made me Real,' said the Skin Horse. 'That was many years ago, but once you're Real, you can't become unreal again. It lasts forever.'

The Rabbit sighed. He thought it would be a long time before the magic called Real happened to him. He longed to become Real, to know what it felt like; yet the idea of growing shabby and losing his eyes and his whiskers was rather sad. He wished he could become Real without those uncomfortable things happening to him."

"But of course he can't," said Bob. "Right?"

"Of course," said Tyler. "Not till his whiskers fall off and his eyes drop out."

"Then, as I recall, when he is properly battered, blind and bald, the Magic Fairy jumps out of a flower, gathers him up in her arms and turns him into Real."

"Just like that."

"And it's all worth it?"

"It's about love," said Tyler. "Real love. There isn't anything else."

"Real love," said Bob.

"Open thy heart, counselor. Let the people in. Surrender."

"Third Step," said Bob. "We did that."

"Ongoing process. Take it into the Eleventh Step. It's your offering to the Force."

"And the Jedi's strength flows from the Force," said Bob.

"Get in touch with it. *Stay* in touch with it."

"*Sought through prayer and meditation to improve . . .*"

"Or establish," cut in Tyler.

"*. . . or establish our conscious contact with the Force.*"

"I do believe you're getting it," said Tyler.

"And I do believe you might be right. Though I'm not sure why."

"No thinking tonight, counselor. Please. Do not, under any circumstances, let the Big Brain play with this one. This is far too important."

"Okay."

"So, in closing, several things. Remember it's the empty space within that makes the vessel useful."

"I'm writing it down," said Bob.

"Urge Father Eddy to just go to meetings for now and not worry about the Hierarchy of Being. If he drinks again he won't have to worry about any of it. And consider making your amends to Beverly. She will make a much better friend than a lover."

"You think?"

"Trust me on this one. How are you and Polly doing?"

"Strange, but we actually seem to be drifting together."

"Good," said Tyler. "I'll leave you with something from St. John of the Cross: 'It is characteristic of the power of love that all things seem possible to it.'"

"The power of love," said Bob. "Why do you suppose we have to go through all this . . . trudgery? You like that word—trudgery? I just made it up. Just now."

"Absolutely amazing," said Tyler.

"Why do you suppose we have to go through all this darkness just to get to—"

"Realize that the dark night of recovery is a gift that has been given to you so that you may share it with others. More will be revealed, counselor. Much more when the time is right."

"All of which leads us to . . . ?"

"To the Twelfth Step and carrying the message," said Tyler. "The Twelfth Step is the final brick in the foundation. The opportunity to be of service is one of the great gifts we are given."

"That and the Dark Night."

"Don't underestimate the value of pain as a learning tool," said Tyler.

"How could I?"

"And since you have not volunteered the information, I will ask. Did you get yourself elected secretary of the Rusty Zipper Group?"

"I did," said Bob. "I'm told it was a landslide."

"You didn't make any campaign promises you can't keep, did you?"

"Like what?"

"Gourmet coffee and jelly doughnuts?"

"No. Although I did consider the jelly doughnuts."

"I'm proud of you," said Tyler.

"Thanks. Part of my duties is to get people to speak at meetings. You available?"

"A distinct possibility."

"Next Thursday?"

"I'll be there."

"And for next time?"

"Watch and wait," said Tyler. "Practice the Eleventh Step. Listen to the silences between words, watch for the empty spaces that are full of magic. You might consider taking in the downtown jail meeting on Saturday night. Call Jake at Central Office. He'll get you in touch with Dick. Might even be a few down there who could use a sponsor."

"Good night, Tyler. Let's call it quits before you find something else for me to do."

Step Twelve

"I got lots of feedback from the guys about your talk at the Zipper meeting," said Bob.

"All good, I hope."

"What else? Funny, the things people think they hear."

"Like what?" said Tyler.

"One guy told me he really liked what you had to say about the Second Step. Far as I know you never even mentioned the Second Step. Another guy told me he loved the story about the parachute. I don't remember a story about a parachute and I was sitting in the front row."

"Paying attention?"

"Of course."

"People hear what they need to hear," said Tyler. "Sometimes I think we could read the phone book at meetings and it would still work. It's not so much the words as it is the process itself. The magic."

"It's very strange sometimes," said Bob, "this process we talk about."

"Very."

"I have some bad news."

"I just got here and already you have bad news?" said Tyler.

"Father Eddy's drinking again."

"That's too bad. When did you see him last?"

"Haven't seen him in maybe a week, but he called a couple of nights ago absolutely smashed. Middle of the night and he's trying to explain the difference between prevenient grace and irresistible grace. At least I think that's what it was. I actually wrote it down, like it might be important."

"There must be a special place in the Kingdom for intellectual drunks," said Tyler. "They have such a hard time of it."

"What should I do?"

"Hope," said Tyler. "Wait. Pray if you're so inclined. Be available. If he calls, ask him if he wants to go to detox. Or to a meeting. Above all, don't try to convince him he ought to get sober. That's his job. Besides, people have been telling him that for years. It never works."

"I finally just hung up on him," said Bob. "I mean, what a jerk. Here he has everything going for him and *zip*, he drinks. Jesus God."

"Not such a big surprise," said Tyler. "It's what drunks do."

"I know, but . . ."

"It's a disease, counselor. Important to remember that. It's not a disease when I have it and a moral weakness when you have it. It's a disease all the time. Or it's not. Any drunk who picks up a drink knowing what's in store for him is not a well person. And the guy who's eating a whole chocolate cake for breakfast? You think he's on the fast track to being okay?"

"Eddy says this recovery stuff just doesn't work for him."

"Another special case," said Tyler.

"Says it's stupid and boring and juvenile. Bunch of drunks sitting around telling each other what terrible people they used to be and how they've found this power that they choose to call God who is working overtime patching up their shabby little lives."

"Priests have a lot of trouble with the God stuff," said Tyler. "They seem to resent the fact that other people have access to this power without all the rigorous training they had to go through. Not only that, but these amateurs are actually trying to give *them* instructions. Doesn't seem at all fair. The French have a saying—or maybe it's the Chinese. Anyway: 'If the cart doesn't go, who do you whip—the cart or the horse?'"

"Meaning?"

"Meaning that there's nothing wrong with the cart. With the process, the program. But it doesn't go—won't go—unless we're willing to get into harness and pull it. Or push it. Unless we're willing to *do* something. Do I hear a call to action here? Father Eddy seems to have piled all this stuff into the cart, then just stood there and watched it. Maybe he expected it to move by itself. Maybe he expected *you* to move it—that's a common misconception about what sponsors are supposed to do."

"Maybe he did," said Bob.

"The process of recovery is the easiest thing in the world

to criticize. If I had to debate pro or con, I would definitely
have to be against. No way this thing can possibly work."

"But it does."

"In defiance of all known rules of logic, it actually does.
Amazing."

"I just hate to see him drinking again. I mean, he was just
getting it together."

"I know," said Tyler. "Perhaps his first insidious brush
with success. That's often when disaster strikes. Seems we
often find it necessary to go into the self-destruct mode
when we're on the brink of having something good happen."

"Why do we do stuff like that?" said Bob. "It just seems
crazy."

"Because it *is* crazy. That's part of the disease. But you
have to stop and think: Why would you do something nice
for someone you didn't like?"

"Like yourself."

"Exactly. All those years trying to destroy myself and now
all of a sudden you want me to do something nice for myself?
To myself? No way, counselor. The enemy is within. Firmly
entrenched. And disguised to boot. He will not be so easily
dislodged. Or found, even."

"Amen."

"So our job is to carry the message," said Tyler, "not the
alcoholic. We are not in the fix-it or transportation business.
Which brings us face to face with the Twelfth Step."

"Which I will now read," said Bob. *"Having had a
spiritual awakening as a result of these steps, we tried
to carry this message to alcoholics, and to practice these
principles in all our affairs."*

"A spiritual awakening as a *result* of these steps," said Tyler.
"Right."
"In *all* our affairs."
"Got it," said Bob.
"I've got a quote here from Albert Schweitzer," said Tyler.
"You're wheeling in the heavy artillery?"
"Right. Time for the big guns. It's the last one, counselor.
Step Twelve. Very important."
"I believe it."
*"I don't know what your destiny will be, but one thing
I do know: The only ones among you who will be truly
happy are those who have sought and learned how to
serve."*
"Carrying the message," said Bob. "I have something from
Pooh. About being together. Maybe about carrying the message. Actually, I'm not even sure it applies, but here it is:
*"'It isn't much fun for One, but Two can stick together,'
says Pooh, says he. 'That's how it is,' says Pooh."*
"I like that," said Tyler. "Two by two, carrying the message,
trudgering the Road of Happy Destiny. Together."
"On our way to the Emerald City, to see the Wizard."
"Just a reminder, counselor. This is the Road *of* Happy
Destiny, not *to* Happy Destiny. Or *to* the Emerald City. It's
not *to* anywhere. It's an *of* road, a be-where-you-are road
that may have direction, but does not necessarily imply a
destination."
"That's very metaphysical, Tyler."
"You're probably right. How about this:
*"Practical experience shows that nothing so much
insures immunity from drinking as intense work with*

other alcoholics."

"Much better," said Bob. "And this: *It works when other activities fail."*

"Also appropriate," said Tyler.

"You think I've had a spiritual awakening?"

"Why are you asking me?"

"Because you're supposed to know."

"It says in the back of one of those books we read that if you've had a personality change sufficient to bring about a recovery from alcoholism, you've had a spiritual awakening."

"That's it?" said Bob. "A personality change? No burning bushes?"

"Hopefully not," said Tyler.

"And here I've been waiting for this big production number with the thunder and lightning and the parting of the clouds and the big bass voice welcoming me to the Promised Land of Spiritual Fulfillment."

"I have a friend I did time with who says his most spiritual experience is waking up in the morning and having the key to the room he's in."

"And yours is realizing that you were just another drunk."

"Right."

"Sounds really exciting," said Bob. "But I'd rather have a burning bush."

"Smoke and mirrors, counselor. High drama. You'll have your share of them, but try not to get hung up on the window dressing. It's not always the best way."

"I want to be rocketed into the fourth dimension. I *yearn* to be rocketed into the fourth dimension."

"Don't we all," said Tyler. "But what will more likely happen is that the day will come when you will realize that your reaction to life has changed. 'Profoundly changed,' as it says, and that the change was not completely your own doing. Your life will be fundamentally changed in ways you will find impossible to describe. You will see another Force at work. Another Power."

"As in Pumpkin Power?" said Bob.

"Could be."

"In the House of the Great Pumpkin there are many mansions."

"Save me a bungalow," said Tyler.

"Consider it done."

"The thing that will strike you most is that what you have managed to give to the process will pale in comparison to what you have received. You suit up, show up, do a few simple things and the world is yours. All yours. On a platter."

"I'll be rich and famous?" said Bob.

"Better than that. You'll be clean and sober. Which means you'll be free. Doesn't get any better than that."

"Ah, freedom."

"Right. Freedom from the bondage of alcohol, drugs, chocolate cake, sex, fear. You name it."

"Heck of a deal."

"One heck of a deal, counselor. If I'm into making deals, this is one I can't pass up. And as an added bonus, nothing can harm you."

"Nothing can harm me?"

"Nothing can harm you," said Tyler.

"Meaning I'll never be sick? I won't die?"

"I didn't say anything about not dying," said Tyler. "I said nothing could *harm* you."

"And dying is like stubbing your toe? One of those no-harm, no-foul deals?"

"Just your body dies, counselor. Not you. You go to another part of the forest."

"I don't get it," said Bob.

"You will," said Tyler. "Give it time."

"And I suppose you know all this from personal experience?"

"Let's just say I've seen the process at work. But then, you have, too."

"How come I don't remember it?"

"You may just have a lousy memory."

"Sometimes you make me crazy, Tyler. You know that?"

"That's good," said Tyler.

"That's good?"

"Crazy wisdom," said Tyler. "The only kind that really makes sense. Tell me more about the Twelfth Step."

"Jesus. Okay: Big Book says that the cornerstone of recovery is being of service."

"Carrying the message," said Tyler. "Now, if reaching out to others is the cornerstone of recovery, what does it say about being successful?"

"It says . . . I don't remember the exact words, but it says something to the effect that it doesn't make any difference if the person you're reaching out to gets sober, or gets the message, or gets anything. The only thing that's important is that you reach out. And by some kind of divine paradox, the giver actually receives."

"Imagine that," said Tyler. "Another paradox. And obviously a learn-by-doing maneuver. Out of the results business and into the Process. Trudgering along, counselor, trudgering along."

"And the magic is the action itself."

"Of course," said Tyler. "Never forget the Magic Factor."

"Making coffee, answering phones, going to meetings, cleaning up—all that stuff is Twelfth-Step work."

"Smiling at people. Wishing them well. Placing them next to your heart. All of it. And most definitely not limited to people in recovery. There is an old English proverb: 'What you deny to others will be denied to you.' You know why that is?"

"Because there aren't any others out there; that's the optical illusion."

"Bravo, counselor. Go to the head of the class. I could kiss you for that."

"That won't be necessary," said Bob.

"Listen to this from the Twelve and Twelve: *Right action is the key to right living.*"

"Very Buddhist," said Bob.

"Very practical," said Tyler.

"This is something we might have found in the Bird Sutra maybe? Or the Cow Sutra?"

"Or the Heart Sutra," said Tyler. "Like the Twelve and Twelve. You remember what language we're using."

"I do," said Bob. "The language of the heart."

"Good. On to the next lesson, which is about being content as long as we *play well whatever cards life deals us.*"

"Even if the best hand you've had for the last couple of months has been a pair of deuces?"

"Especially if that's the case," said Tyler.

"And what happens if we don't play it—the hand?"

"Well, if we just hold it and don't play it, don't even tell anyone about it, we get to keep the same hand day after day after day after day. Same lousy hand. As a matter of fact, we get to keep it till we get *willing* to play it."

"There's that word *willing* again," said Bob. "What about the good hands?"

"You kidding?" said Tyler. "You ever see a drunk who didn't want to play a good hand? Try and stop him."

"So if you play the hand you've got, even if it's lousy, you get another one the next day?"

"Guaranteed," said Tyler. "You know, I've had days when a pair of deuces would've looked great."

"Me, too."

"There's a very important universal law that's an equation. It goes like this: No action equals no change. Simple. So, you play the hand. You move the cart. You just do it. Because if you don't, nothing will happen. Ever. Paralysis will set in and you will become a statue. A monument. A pigeon rest. You will be left to lament the present and the awful hand life has dealt you. 'Poor me,' you'll say. 'Poor me. Pour me a drink.'"

"I see how that can happen."

"And does," said Tyler. "More often than we like to think. Now love, counselor, is an action. Love is talking to the guy who wants to start on his second chocolate cake at 7 A.M., or the guy who thinks that just one drink won't hurt. Love is making coffee at the Rusty Zipper Group."

"And Beverly? What was she?"

"Beverly was an interlude. Perhaps a pleasant one. But

don't mistake it for the real thing. Here's what Teilhard de Chardin says about—"

"Who?"

"A French priest. Jesuit."

"Not a Bird Sutra guy?"

"No," said Tyler. "This is what he said about love: *"Someday, after we have mastered the winds, the waves, the tides and gravity, we will harness for God the energies of love. Then, for the second time in the history of the world, Mankind will have discovered fire."*

"This what we have here?" said Bob. "Fire?"

"It is," said Tyler. "We have discovered fire. Again."

"This like the Holy Spirit deal? Tongues of fire?"

"More like *The Velveteen Rabbit*," said Tyler. "The Skin Horse. Pooh. Yoda. Real lovers."

"The real lovers are in children's stories?" said Bob.

"Most of them."

"Funny, the things you never think about," said Bob. "Like the children's stories. And the stuff we've been through the last few months. You and me. And somehow it's changed me. I don't know how, but it has. I didn't know about this stuff; hardly any of it. Never would have found out if I hadn't been in such a bad place."

"Three cheers for desperation," said Tyler. "Doesn't Shakespeare say something about the sweet uses of adversity?"

"Close to a drink. Maybe closer than I thought. I was actually reduced to asking for help."

"The bottom," said Tyler. "Surrender time. When the student is ready, the teacher will appear. Never fails."

"I don't know," said Bob. "I've seen guys in terrible shape who just went back to drinking and using. Walked out the door and never came back. Weren't they ready? Maybe there weren't any teachers available."

"And maybe they just had more drinking and using to do, counselor. A few more chocolate cakes, a little more sexual degradation, one more bone to stroke. Grist for the mill. Lessons. There are always plenty of teachers. If we're short of anything, it's students."

"So some people just aren't ready?"

"Some never *get* ready."

"Wonder why?" said Bob. "They don't hurt enough?"

 "Hardly that," said Tyler. "The nature of the disease is to tell you that you don't have it, to tell you that everything is just fine as your life goes spiraling down the drain."

"So long, Life."

"Some of us continue to look for other ways out of the dilemma. Some say there are easier, softer ways, but I doubt that. Half measures usually don't work for us. I do know it takes a great deal of courage to walk into those rooms and reveal yourself to people you don't know. Drunks. Addicts. God knows what else. Misfits, you think, people from the side of the tracks you've been trying to avoid all your life."

Tyler's voice took on a faraway quality. "It isn't till later that you realize that they're just like you. Or that you're just like them. Initially all you know is that your ass is exposed and you're quite sure everyone is going to make fun of you because not only is your ass hanging out there for everyone to see, but you are about to reveal the fact that you don't have a clue about how to live life without drugs and alcohol, or a dozen doughnuts for breakfast, or betting a hundred dollars a day that you don't have on baseball games that you don't care about."

[A two-second pause, then the scraping of a chair and Tyler resumed.]

"My sponsor had this One-Door Theory. If you wanted to live, if you wanted to truly recover from whatever addiction was controlling your life, there was just one door that you opened. Just one. There wasn't one marked Love, one marked Happiness, one marked Fear and so forth. There was just one door marked Life, and when you opened it you got hit in the face with the whole thing, the whole mixed bag. Welcome to earth, pilgrim. Don't underestimate the amount of courage it takes to open the door, to leave it open. And don't waste time judging those who don't. Everybody really is doing the best they can. Why some people make it and some don't is one of life's great mysteries. But this is not about good or bad or judgment or a cosmic point total. It's about life. And your job in all this, counselor, is to do what?"

"I got this one down pat," said Bob. "My job is to carry the message. Maybe *be* the message."

"And not to worry about who gets it and who doesn't. That's not your business."

"Because I'm not in the results business. Not even a little bit."

"Right. You're in the . . . what business?"

"I'm in the suit-up-and-show-up business," said Bob.

"Good."

"I've been reading Walt Whitman."

"Oh?" said Tyler.

"Surprised?"

"Only a little."

"This is from *Leaves of Grass:*

"*I hear and behold God in every object, yet understand
God not in the least. . . .*

*I see something of God in each hour of the twenty-four,
and each moment.*

*In the faces of the men and women I see God and in my
own face in the glass,*

*I find letters from God dropped in the street, and every
one is signed with God's name,*

*And I leave them where they are, for I know that wher-
ever I go,*

Others will punctually come, for ever and ever."

"You have come a long way, counselor."

"You think?"

"You have traveled the longest distance on earth—the distance from your head to your heart."

"I've arrived?"

"Careful with the terminology," said Tyler. "'Arrived'
makes it sound like there's some destination you get to so
you can rest."

"No resting?"

"None. Traveling from your head to your heart brings with
it the realization that you are connected to everything and
everyone. That's the message of the heart. The mind separates, the heart unites."

"Less thinking and more loving?"

"Definitely," said Tyler. "The heart sees life from a
different vantage point. The illusion of separation will fall

away, and you will realize that all those people out there—
the good, the bad, the saints and the sinners—all of them are
your brothers and sisters, parts of the same Great Spirit who
have come to share the journey with you. And there are no
mistakes, counselor—only lessons."

"Jesus."

"And with that I will say farewell," said Tyler. "I have no
speeches left. No words."

"You mean this is it? We won't meet again?" Bob sounded
startled.

"Not for a while."

"I'll see you at meetings?"

"Doubtful," said Tyler. "I have other . . . commitments."

"What do I do now?" said Bob, his voice rising slightly.

"Whatever you want," said Tyler. "You're free. That's what
this is all about. Test your wings; that's the first thing most
butterflies do. Go find Eddy and tell him you love him."

"Eddy's probably drunk."

"All the more reason," said Tyler.

"Where will I find him?"

"Look in your heart. That's where everything is."

"Jesus. This stuff just blows me away."

"Listen to the wind, to the whispers. Listen to the
children. To the voices. If you are quiet, you will hear them.
Carry the message, counselor. I can see the changes."

"You can?"

"You can, too. Just close your eyes for a moment. Many
have gathered to be a part of that change. This is not only
about people in recovery—although we are a likely group
simply because our various addictions have driven us either

into the grave or into a state of reasonableness, thereby making us a little more teachable. Pain is a great equalizer in that sense. But this is about everyone. The teachers are coming now. The students are being readied."

"It's about love, isn't it?" said Bob. "All of it."

"Plain and simple," said Tyler. "Life turns out to be an affair of the heart."

"This is a little awkward," said Bob, "but I want to say it anyway." (The sound of a throat clearing.) "I love you. It's not like I—"

"Don't explain," said Tyler. "I understand."

"I just wanted to say that. Wanted you to know."

"Thank you."

"We're really done?"

"For now," said Tyler. "But it's never really done. It just goes on."

"What does?"

"Everything."

"Can I call you?" said Bob.

"I'll be . . . traveling mostly."

"How am I going to get in touch with you?"

"You know your morning meditation?"

"Sure."

"Ask," said Tyler.

"Ask what?" said Bob. "To get in touch with you? Who do I ask?"

"You could try the Force. Or the Great Pumpkin. Or God even. Doesn't make any difference as long as you ask; that's the important part. The names are just names."

"And you'll know?"

"I'll know."

"How in the world will you—"

"Don't complicate it," said Tyler. "Your job is to just ask."

"More will be revealed?"

"It will."

"I hope. Anyway, I'm really going to miss you."

"I won't be far away. Give my best to Polly and Donna. Go find Father Eddy. I see him singing High Mass at St. John's someday, but now he is lonely and frightened. He waits to be found. He would call out but he has no voice. Go find him and be his voice for now. Good-bye, counselor. Till we meet again. Happy trudgering. My best to Pooh if you see him."

"You think that's possible?" said Bob. "Me running into Pooh someday?"

"Anything's possible," said Tyler. "We're both clean and sober. What are the odds against that?"

"Right," said Bob. "I'll keep my eyes open."

"And your heart."

"Of course. And my heart. Good night, Tyler."

"Good night, counselor. See you on the other side."

And that's where the tape ended.

WORKS CITED

Anonymous. *Alcoholics Anonymous*. New York: Alcoholics Anonymous World Services, Inc., 1955.

Bach, Richard. *Illusions/Adventures of a Reluctant Messiah*. New York: Delacorte Press, 1977.

Baum, L. Frank. *The Wizard of Oz*. New York: Holt, Rinehart & Winston, 1982.

Carroll, Lewis. *Alice's Adventures in Wonderland*. Philadelphia: The John Winston Co., 1923

Eliot, T. S. *Collected Poems 1909–1935*. New York: Harcourt, Brace, 1936.

Ellis, Havelock. *The Dance of Life*. Boston: Houghton Mifflin, 1923.

Gibran, Kahlil. *The Prophet*. New York: A. A. Knopf, 1923.

Glut, Donald F. *Star Wars Trilogy: The Empire Strikes Back*. New York: Ballantine Books, 1987.

Higgins, John. *Thomas Merton on Prayer*. New York: Doubleday, 1973.

James, William. *Varieties of Religious Experience*. New York: Collier, 1961.

Kabir. *Songs of Kabir from the Adi Granth*. New York: State University of New York Press, 1991.

Kahn, James. *Star Wars Trilogy: Return of the Jedi.* New York: Ballantine Books, 1987.

Lao Tzu. *Tao Teh Ching.* Boston: Shambhala, 1989.

Merton, Thomas. *The Seven Story Mountain.* New York: Harcourt, Brace, 1948.

Milne, A. A. *Now We Are Six.* New York: E. P. Dutton, 1954.

——. *The World of Pooh: Complete Winnie-the-Pooh and the House at Pooh Corner.* New York: E. P. Dutton, 1957.

Paulus, Trina. *hope for the flowers.* New York: Paulist Press, 1972.

Rumi. *Open Secret: Versions of Rumi.* Putney, Vt.: Threshold Books, 1984.

Schulz, Charles. *Happy Holloween.* New York: HarperCollins, 1994.

Teilhard de Chardin, Pierre. *Phenomenon of Man.* New York: Harper & Brothers, 1959.

Whitman, Walt. *Leaves of Grass.* New York: Doubleday, Doran & Co., Inc., 1940.

Williams, Margery. *The Velveteen Rabbit.* New York: Holt, Rinehart & Winston , 1983.

Williams, Paul. *Das Energi.* New York: Warner Books, 1978.

ABOUT THE AUTHOR

Edward Bear is a pseudonym. The author was born in Brooklyn, New York and grew up in Los Angeles, California. His early adventures included a brief stint in minor-league baseball, as well as too many years in construction, day labor and other dead-end jobs. He attended six different colleges but received no degrees. A correspondence course in engineering landed him a job at Hewlett-Packard, where he has been employed for nearly thirty years.

He has published several fiction pieces in small literary magazines and a novel, *Diamonds Are Trumps* (St. Luke's Press, 1990). He currently lives with his wife high in the Rocky Mountains, where he plays a vintage Martin guitar and writes in whatever time the gods and goddesses have left for him.

Made in the USA
Las Vegas, NV
09 June 2021

24470071R00115